Dear [Amy],

I hope that you
enjoy this, my
latest work.
-- And if you do,
please spread
the word.
All Best,

[signature]

MW00592754

LETTERS *to a*

YOUNG HEALER

DAVID SHUCH

RIVER GROVE
BOOKS

Published by River Grove Books
Austin, TX
www.rivergrovebooks.com

Distributed by River Grove Books

Design and composition by Greenleaf Book Group
Cover design by Greenleaf Book Group
Cover images used ©iStockphoto.com/CSA Images and latsun
Author photo by Mary Shuch

Publisher's Cataloging-in-Publication data is available.

Trade Paperback ISBN: 978-1-63299-168-3

Hardcover ISBN: 978-1-63299-169-0

eBook ISBN: 978-1-63299-170-6

First Edition

 For MARY

AUTHOR'S NOTE

After the passing of my dear friend Madeline, a trove of correspondence was discovered in the drawer of her writing desk. This consisted of twelve hand-written letters from her uncle James that had arrived over the course of a single year when she must have been about eighteen. The letters provide no dates, but strangely, each bears the month in which it was written: the first one in January and the last, in December.

I can't be certain of her exact age when she and James corresponded, but when she was near the end of her life, she asked me to transcribe her recollections from the time of her apprenticeship with Simon, the charm carver, which was then published as *The Charm Carver* (Integrative Arts Press, 2005). And it is clear from the contents of these letters that this correspondence occurred some years after that apprenticeship, which ended when she was sixteen.

I found these letters to be a remarkable exposition on the subject of healing. A subject that was central in her life.

Other than my indicating on the Contents page my sense of the main themes covered in each letter and the footnotes marking the page numbers from *The Charm Carver* that correspond to items mentioned in these letters, I have not added or changed a single word from James' original correspondence.

Contents

On Love

My Dearest Madeline,

Praise be to God! For more years than I can count, I prayed in secret for you—ardently, fervently—that you would blossom despite the strikes against you. But now, know that even from the day you were born, I have felt in my heart a deep love for you. In ways we can never fully grasp, souls are often drawn by a feeling of another. And it was just this kind of unknowable thing that drew my heart to you. How I wished I could have helped you in your formative years, but alas, that was impossible.

Your father and I, though brothers, never did see

eye to eye. He always felt at home in our society, while I was at odds with the elders.[1] And so, he pushed me away from any influence I might have had with you or your brother.[2] But in my heart, I have always wished you well, and now you are no longer a child and have, to my delight, taken it upon yourself to write to me for advice! I will help you in any way that I can.

From reading your letter, I sense that your mind is a jumble. It may surprise you, but I could not imagine that it would be otherwise right now. Your apprenticeship with that remarkable fellow taught you much that is at odds with all that you learned in your youth. After all, how could a man carving stones[3] bring people healing? And if this is possible, what does that mean? Perhaps you are even more confused that I would have any sense of what you are going through? I take this as a sign to share a secret that up until now I have never revealed.

Before I became a doctor, I worked in a quarry, mining blocks of stone.[4] I befriended a man nearly

---

1   *The Charm Carver*, p 13.
2   Ibid., p 55.
3   Ibid., p 11.
4   Ibid., p 87.

twice my age, who was widely regarded as strange, but he seemed to me as a saint disguised. His name was Simon, and I couldn't understand his presence. He was the oldest one there but stronger than three. And quiet . . . so very quiet as he worked. I remember his eyes. His gaze was never rushed or flitting; it was patient and deep. I asked him what brought him to this line of work, and he told me that he had always loved stones and wished to learn about them "in their homes." To him, this job was part of his schooling.

We kept in touch after leaving the quarry, and he told me about his trade. When your father died, I asked Simon if he might carve a charm for you. I told him that he could not reveal that he even knew me, as your mother and the elders would send him away. He looked into my eyes for a very long time and finally said, "I will go to her, but don't tell me her name." It seemed a strange request, but I heard he had no trouble finding you.[5]

And so, my dear, now you know. I never got a chance to thank him for all he did, and now he is long gone, except in our recollections and, of course, in his

---

5   *The Charm Carver*, p 11.

charms. But as with you, much of my understanding comes from my time with him, and if you wish, we may reminisce!

Your loving uncle,

James

On Intentionality

My Dearest Madeline,

I was delighted to hear back from you so soon following my last letter. But oh, you seem so fretful of what you shall do over this decision in front of you! If I may once again offer you some advice, it is this: Don't fret! If you wish to carry a spirit of healing within you, it makes little difference what field you choose, as there is so much healing that needs to be done—in every realm and to every degree! Work does not exist where bringing to it a spirit of healing will not weave your efforts in with the divine. And what is healing but drying a tear in the eye of God?

Among the true healers, I have known not one who would call themselves a healer. They would blush at their work being thought of this way; none see what they do through this lens, and few ever make a study of healing, but healers they are—one and all! But you, with your curious mind, may wish to learn about what healing is and what it can be. Such learning helps anyone be more effective, but it is not at all necessary. Let me tell you about three people I have known who bring a healing spirit into their work, yet none of them have studied healing.

Years ago, I moved to a different country. The change in my surroundings gave me an anxious feeling in the pit of my stomach, and I became more nervous than I had ever been in my life. I could not attribute this nervousness to anything other than my move, and I hoped the feelings would pass as time went on. But instead, they intensified, and I thought that I might have to move to yet a different country.

In my new neighborhood, there was a bakery I went to for bread. I never saw the baker, but he made a simple loaf, and I bought one every day. One day, this bakery happened to be closed, and I walked to the next neighborhood and found a new bakery. Here, I saw the baker working at his dough. He was a quiet man with a warm smile but not given to many words. His loafs were also simple and looked identical to the ones that I had gotten at the other establishment. This loaf, I found out, was made in all of the bakeries in this country, and all were made the same way with the same ingredients. I took one home and had it with my breakfast. Its texture was a bit finer, but otherwise, it tasted the same as the other loaf. Yet a short time later, I noticed that my nervousness was gone, but I didn't attribute this to anything in particular. I first thought nothing of it and went on with my day, figuring that I was finally getting used to my surroundings.

This calmer feeling stayed with me that whole day. The next morning, I rose and went back to my local bakery, which had reopened, and there, I bought bread for breakfast. As soon as I ate it, the nervousness returned! I didn't make a connection until the next day when this bakery was again closed, and I went back to the other one, and after eating that bread, I felt so very good again.

The first bakery never reopened. A notice in the newspaper explained that the baker there, who was known as an angry man, had killed his wife in a fit of rage! Perhaps he was nursing grudges while he was kneading his dough, and something of this got baked into his loaves?

It still did not explain the good feelings I got from eating the other bread. But as I got to know this other baker and got him to open up a bit, he shared with me so that I came to understand. I asked him about his work, and he replied that he gave enormous respect to the dough. "I don't rush it; it is a living thing," he said. "When I knead it, it speaks to me, not in words but in how it responds to my hands. I must be quiet to listen, so I never engage in conversation while I am with the dough. It lets me know how much to knead it, how to handle it, and when I should stop and let it rest. Then I just bake it, and it becomes bread."

And in some way and without trying, this baker imbued his calm and deliberate spirit into his creations and produced bread that took away nervousness, and not just in me. He always had a line of people stretched down the block of his shop, and as I waited with them and spoke with many, I found that mine was a shared experience.

But he never called himself a healer.

The next person I will tell you about I met while

spending a few days with your cousin while she was working at the local animal shelter. Among her assignments was trying to adopt out a young, male cat that had been born with an affliction affecting his balance. Unlike most cats, which possess a sense of grace as they move, this one walked and moved awkwardly. And though this fellow lacked other problems, he had been returned three times by different families for reasons ascribed to allergies.

The cat, lacking the cuteness of a kitten and having the baggage of three failed adoptions and his awkward gait, was considered difficult to place. Over many months, no one expressed interest in adopting him, and I was told several had snickered at his gait.

Then one day, a woman arrived looking for a cat. She was curious about this one with its odd manner of getting around. She did not fawn over him or take pity on him. It seemed as if she felt pity to be beneath him. He sat on her lap, purring, while a kind of communion seemed to pass between them.

After a time, the woman got up and left the adoption floor. As your cousin was walking her out, the woman told her that she would return in seven days to adopt this cat and to please be sure that no one else adopted him first. Your cousin was surprised by the request, as no one had given this cat a second look, but the woman had been adamant. So paperwork was put in place. I happened to be visiting her again the following week when this woman returned. Your cousin then told me that six separate individuals over the previous week had wanted to adopt this very cat. The shelter had never had so much interest in an animal designated hard to place before. The only explanation was that the cat knew that he had found his home, and this healed him in a way that made him stand out.

Your cousin shared this turn of events with the woman. Then I introduced myself, and I asked if she could shed light on what had happened to this cat. She looked at me for what seemed a long time. Finally, she said, "I'm not surprised by what happened; that's why I insisted that no one be allowed to adopt him until I could return. He knew I loved him and would always love him, and that is all he needed; he's really no different than you and me."

I learned that in the days after the woman first came, the little cat's countenance changed. His eyes, dull before, now held sparks, and his sad state transformed to a bright and sweet disposition. In the shelter, it was said that he began to look like an angel of God.

But this woman would never call herself a healer.

The last person I want to tell you about is a cleaning lady. A good friend of mine is a psychologist who specializes in treating women who have been abused. He works out of two consultation rooms at the end of a hallway: one on the left and one on the right. The rooms are identical—the same furniture, the same lighting—so that a fragile client, struggling with emotional release, would not be thrown off by a different setting, week to week.

But my friend was perplexed. For a reason he could not explain, his clients all wished to be seen only in the room to the right. When he asked them why, many couldn't even answer or simply said, "I feel more comfortable in the room on the right; I don't know why."

Knowing of my interest in these kinds of things, he asked me to investigate, and I first went into each room and confirmed that they were indeed neat, clean, and identical. I asked him if he knew of anything that was different between the two rooms. He thought about this for a long time and then said, "Well, they are each cleaned by a different cleaning lady. And each lady always cleans the same room." So I asked if I could meet these two ladies, and it was arranged.

I observed both of them and found a small difference in their approach to their work. The one who cleaned the room on the left listened to music with a rapid beat, and this seemed to make the job more pleasant for her. She worked quickly and in time with her music. The one who cleaned the room to the right did not listen to music and seemed more intent on her cleaning.

Then I asked each lady how they knew that their room was done—how did they each determine that their room was clean? The lady who cleaned the room on the left told me, "This room takes me fifteen minutes to clean. I look at my watch, and I know I'm done when that amount of time has passed." The lady who cleaned the room on the right told me something else. "Oh, when I first go into that room I get a feeling in my chest—like a heavy weight, and I feel very bad— sad and angry; why, I don't know. So, I clean, really, to get rid of this feeling, and when it is gone, I know that the room is clean!"

There was one more curious detail about these two rooms. It may seem like a small thing, but it brings up a big subject that, if you are interested, we can cover at another time. I visited this office on a cold winter evening, and I happened to notice that the picture window in each was covered with frost. I have always been fascinated by patterns made by nature, so it was natural for me to study the crystallizations in the frost. The patterns on the window in the room to the left were sharp and jagged, like the appearance of broken glass. The patterns on the window in the room to the right looked like bunches and bunches of chrysanthemums.

Can you imagine how the work of these cleaning ladies might affect the patterns of frost on the outsides of windows? Soon after my observation of the two women, my psychiatrist friend began to insist that the cleaning service only send him this one lady who had such a beneficial effect on the room to the right.

But she would never call herself a healer.

And so, my dear, ponder in your heart what healing can mean. There are many realms and many degrees of healing, and one day, you will find your way. But don't fret! If you begin to feel that a path before you is too big and too much of a burden, it only means it is worthy. And for that burden, you can do much to prepare.

But how to prepare? That is a big subject, and if you are interested, we can cover it at another time. And we can, if you wish, with that curious mind of yours, dive deeply into the workings of healing itself. I look forward to hearing from you!

Your loving uncle,

James

On Realms of Healing

My Dearest Madeline,

I see that I have piqued your interest in learning more about the realms and degrees of healing, all of which are a comfort to God! The degrees will have to wait, as they are a big subject, but there are only three realms, and when the time comes for you to choose your work, you will find your place among them; everyone with a heart for healing always finds their place.

No one realm is better than another; they are equal in the eyes of God, and work in one does not rule out work in another. Some kinds of work lend themselves to just a single realm, others two realms, and others all three. The realms are like ingredients in a stew! If you pick a carrot out of the pot, will you not also taste a bit of onion? If you find someone professing their own chosen realm to be elevated above the others, he reveals himself as a false healer. Perhaps you would like to learn about them? But that is also a big subject and, for now, will have to wait. Any ordinary occupation can be elevated to include a spirit of healing, but no occupation requires it, though some would seem an empty shell if they did not contain some element of this spirit in them.

But just because a kind of work lends itself to a kind of healing does not obligate a worker to go this extra mile. Indeed, I believe that it is a calling to do this something extra. It has to come from something very deep. Simon called it an *inner wish*[6] ... maybe he shared this with you?

One realm involves healing through substances, objects, and structures where some thing is conditioned in a particular way and serves as a kind of storage device that holds a spirit of healing in the same way as a bell holds its ring. Here you will find those,

---

6   *The Charm Carver*, p 59.

like Simon,[7] who work in crafts or art or like the baker who made those loaves of bread that I loved so much. But also those who design, build, and, like the cleaning lady, maintain the spaces that we occupy.

Another realm involves healing without physical contact or intervening objects, and this includes healing through prayer, diplomacy, and relationships and also through words, poetry, and music. For example, throughout my many years of education, I encountered a few teachers who, through example, encouragement, and assignment, helped my young soul to heal in more ways than I can count.

Perhaps you think I am just speaking about those who showed me compassion? Having a heart of compassion is the most important thing, and in truth, few who bring a spirit of healing into their work ever think about it, let alone study it. But for those, like you, born with a compassionate heart and an ache to understand what lies at the heart of healing, there can be no path in life more fulfilling than bringing this spirit into your work. Think of this as tuning your instrument.

The last realm involves healing through some kind

---

7   Ibid., p 17.

of contact with the body—where the healing spirit, itself a kind of love from above, passes through this contact. In truth, there are times when healing in the prior realm, particularly in one-on-one conversations held within a close relationship, can have all the characteristics of this realm; the only difference is that the contact there just involves a meeting of the minds and hearts, whereas here, bodies meet as well.

Today I will tell you about three people who heal in this realm. And while outwardly, their forms of contact are quite common, their results are each unique. And this will get us started on this wider subject that interests you so much—what is healing? Here we have three people who heal by giving a kiss or a hug.

The first person is your own mother. Though my contact with you and your family stopped when you were very young, I was present when you were learning to walk. One day, you fell down and skinned your knee and began to cry. Your mother picked you up and kissed your knee, and instantly, your crying stopped. Your knee still had a bruise, and I'm sure that it still hurt, but your mother's kiss changed your whole experience.

You knew that everything was going to be all

right, even though at that young age you had no idea what *everything* even meant! And while an unwanted kiss from a stranger may have made you cry more, this kiss from your mother—conveying her love for you and your trusting of her—brought you a different experience, one where you could see, maybe for the first time, that with a bit of help you could rise above this challenge.[8]

The jumble of spirits jarred within you by your fall were put back in their places by your mother's kiss. This reordering of spirits is one kind of healing. Normally it is the job of the soul to curate and cultivate the spirits that indwell within it—holding some tightly and others loosely. But at that tender age when you skinned your knee, your soul was not yet formed enough, not yet strong enough to do this work on its own, except in the gentlest of circumstances.

How fortunate for you that you had the love of your mother to do what parental love is supposed to do—curate and cultivate your soul so that, in time, it would become strong enough to curate and cultivate the spirits that animate you.

---

8   *The Charm Carver*, p 86.

It was hard for your soul to lose your father while you were so young. It left a breach that left you yearning; how fortunate it was for you that Simon found you and was able to help you heal.[9]

Some are not as fortunate as you, my dearest niece! When a mother's love is absent or worse, when the mother is nefarious, the soul must learn the hard way how to nourish itself and how to relate to women— tasks that, instead of taking the few years of childhood, can take decades. When the father's love is absent or worse, the soul must learn the hard way how to protect itself and how to relate to men, which instead of taking a few years of childhood, can also take decades.[10]

It is a fact of our existence that any realm amenable to bringing in a spirit of healing can even more easily serve as a conduit for its opposite as with arrogance substituting for compassion. How much easier is it to be arrogant than to be compassionate? This is for the same reason that the opposite of compassion is arrogance; how much easier is it to be arrogant than to be compassionate? Everything depends upon intent, strength of awareness, and integrity to be in accord

---

9   The Charm Carver, p 89.
10   Ibid., pp 59-61.

with the highest kind of love. Ah, but these are big subjects! And they will have to wait.

The next person I will tell you about is a police officer, who saw a young man threaten an old woman with a knife, snatch her bag, and knock her to the ground. The young man broke into a run, and the policeman gave chase and caught him. It would be expected for a policeman in this circumstance to be rough on this criminal. But in this particular case, the policeman, who was a muscular man, caught the thief in a bear hug and held him fast. Now this hug itself could have been violent, especially as the thief had a knife, but the officer told me that in that instant he felt compassion for this poor soul. It was not sympathy—this man had just committed a violent crime—but compassion without sympathy, and he simply held this thief in his massive arms until a moment passed and all the fight went out of him.

Now seems as good a time as any to comment on the differences between these two feelings. Rare is a distinction made between compassion and sympathy, but they are as different as a tree and a bird. A tree makes no sound of its own—only the wind can cause it to rustle. And it stands, grounded and tall and strong enough to weather storms. A bird freely shares its feeling in song, yet it has no root, no grounding other than the wind, which can blow it this way and that.

The officer told me that he had the strangest feeling that this thief, in that instant, seemed to be relieved that he was caught. It was as if the poor fellow's soul had, at that instant, glimpsed a glow of conscience thanks to this unexpected and undeserved consolation. The whole thing could have ended with bloodshed had it not been for the fleeting wave of compassion that passed between the officer and the thief.

But this police officer would never call himself a healer! Yet compassion, particularly when undeserved, can open a heart to a wider, less self-serving perspective. This is another kind of healing.

The third person I will tell you about is a woman with a particular gift with hugs. She herself had been healed of her brokenness solely through the power of love. And so out of her now more perfect heart, she gives a sense of this to those who are most dear to her.

I have always been fascinated by the diversity of experience within the expression of hugs. There are hugs that are superficial, with no real exchange except the empty social ritual, and in this sense, they can be tiresome.

In others, an exchange occurs, of which there are five distinct types. In the first, one gives something unwanted to the other. In the second, one takes something not offered from the other. The last three are the more helpful kinds of hugs. In the third type of hug, one permits the taking of whatever is needed (where there is an abundance to give). In the fourth, one gives where there is a sensed need, but the recipient is too proud, shy, or fearful to take that which will be of most help to them.

In the fifth kind, in accord with the highest kind of love, there forms an exchange that transcends any sense of giving or receiving, where two souls briefly mingle and form a channel for something higher to flow in. And while it would seem to be common sense that for this kind of exchange both participants would need to bring equal degrees of intent, strength, and integrity to the occasion, this is not at all how healing works.

Do you know that if you place a magnet against a piece of iron, the iron becomes magnetized, but the original magnet loses none of its strength? Or in a classroom full of children sitting every which way, if one who is widely respected sits up straight, compelling others to sit up as well, this act will not in any way diminish the posture of the first child. Rather, it will encourage the first child to sit up even straighter. So it is with healing. It is never a matter of energy expended and lost, but rather, it is a matter of creating and holding an alignment that opens a window to heaven.

Finding one who can bring this about is a rare thing, and little of the experience can be put into words. But there are features of this exchange that are important for you to know, as they are important aspects of healing.

The experience is always diverse—things happen on different levels all at the same time, like a symphony where melodies are harmonized in different octaves, pulling the listener's ear this way and that. The first part of the experience is a silencing of the inner talk that is always at play in the mind. Then a sense of timelessness sets in. And then comes a kind of grand exchange—with, on one level, feelings of trust and acceptance and, on another level, feelings that can be described as a kindredness of souls. On a third level is a feeling of fullness in the heart that persists even hours after the embrace, leaving a kind of remembrance. Typical of this encounter, the soul gains courage and fortitude. Bringing to another this taste of the love of God is yet another kind of healing.

Throughout history and even in our own time, there are holy people who heal all that come to them in precisely this way. This woman who heals in this way does not live as a saint but leads the life of a normal person, with a job, a spouse, and a family. Her gift is constrained to those in her life that she holds most dear. And that brings up the final point that I will make to you in this letter—as there are different realms of healing, there are also different degrees. In this kind of healing, some are given to bring this spirit to thousands, others to hundreds, others to dozens, others to just a few, and others to only one. In the eyes of God, there is no difference among them. And this woman would never call herself a healer.

Well enough, my sweet niece. I have taken up much of your time with my ramblings—write soon, and let me know if you have any questions.

Your loving uncle,

James

On False Healers

My Dearest Madeline,

Well then . . . it seems we have a bit of unpleasantness
to go through. But fear not! No subject so close to God
can have only sweetness and light. For heaven did not
bring us into creation to satisfy our every whim, nor
were we destined to exist as just automatons, without
chance of novelty or choice. What benefit could there
be for God to create just a predetermined mechanism?

We have been given this life in order to make
choices, and the ones that are most profound for our
souls present us with one path that will guarantee our
own satisfaction regardless of the consequences for

others and a second path that offers no such guarantee but creates a chance, but only a chance, for improving the lot of another.

The first path is so very popular today, and it is ascribed only to selfishness, but I trace its roots to the dawn of our age, when science, for what was then a good reason, divorced itself from any connection with heaven, except in the most mechanical sense. The fruit of this tree has legitimized within our lives the dismissal of any profound connection that links us to others and to the larger brilliance of heaven. And nowhere does this matter more than within the work of healing. So your question about false healers brings up the topic of those who work from this point of view—without sense of a higher connection, they see their life as nothing more than a path to assure their own gain.

Now I must be careful in my words to you, so that you have a clear idea of a fine distinction. There is an enormous benefit to your soul in pursuing the work that we are communicating about. And there is nothing wrong and, indeed, much that is right and good in following this path. But these benefits are of a different order, a higher order than are the benefits that are pursued by false healers.

For them, there is a cold satisfaction from having their way with people, who they don't really care about except in so far as those individuals can be useful to them. For them, there is never any sense of risk to themselves, as they will always make sure that they land on top.

But the satisfaction that comes from the work that I am sharing with you comes from the sense that, through your efforts, God will feel closer for those who encounter your work, and this is not without risk. There is no shortage of martyrs who have lost their lives for this very reason! But there are more common risks—risks of opening yourself up and getting hurt; risks of disappointment, loss, and grief; risks of failure despite monumental efforts; and risks of social isolation. Look what happened to me, how the elders, tied as they are to the prevailing winds of science, and sadly, your father also, shunned me. And had they learned of Simon's work and his influence on you, they would have chased him away and punished you![11] This work carries a worldview that many find deeply threatening. But that is another subject and best left for another day.

---

11   *The Charm Carver*, p 13.

You must guard yourself from false healers and be aware that it is easier to spot them when they are someone you meet than when any one of them is a small inclination within your own heart. Everything is a matter of degree, my dear, so know that part of your work will require a regular housecleaning within your inner chambers, as even a trace of the tendencies that I am about to describe can, as it were, sour your milk.

False healers come in three types, and although you may find combinations of these three, there is usually one type that will stand out, high and proud, in any given false healer. Two types are easy to spot; the third takes a bit of sensitivity because this type doesn't so much appear to be a certain way but rather the atmosphere around them has a certain feel. And it will be important for you to develop a sensitivity for the atmospheres around people, but how to do that is a subject that will have to wait for another day.

Let me tell you about three false healers, each one of which embodies one of these types.

The first was a man who called himself a healer. He worked with the energies of the body and had some skill in manipulating them. But as he did so, his central wish was not for the well-being of his clients, although he pretended as though it were, but instead, his wish was to be admired for his great skill, his great sensitivity, and his great power. In short, the axis of his being held a wish for adulation, even worship.

A test for this came during a session when a client asked him a question that, owing to his very thin skin, he took as a challenge to his judgment. In an instant, his serene countenance dropped like a mask, and, in anger, he stormed out of the room like an actor exiting his stage. The poor patient, having been opened by his preliminary work, was now left to put herself back together without any sense of what had just happened.

Now it must be said that in life you will meet many who regard themselves above all others and wish for the world to revolve around them. And though they are selfish in this way, at least they are honest and forthright about it. This is not true for a false healer, who shares this same inner tendency yet uses his relationships with those he professes to help in order to extract an extra measure of that which feeds him. Once again, we will have to leave this topic of what feeds the soul for another day—a big topic indeed!

All healing orbits, like a planet, around the sun of

compassion. In this work, it is as if the main spirit in the center of the soul, around which all the other spirits organize themselves, is this very spirit of compassion. It connects us, like a ray, all the way up to heaven. If, instead of compassion, the central axis is arrogance, then there will be no possibility of bringing the energies of heaven into the picture. An arrogant spirit stands in direct opposition to a compassionate spirit. Arrogance keeps the channel between us and what is higher closed and sealed, and compassion helps hold the channel open. So beware of this first type of false healer, whose soul harbors an arrogant spirit.

Now seems as good a time as any to comment on the subject of payment, because this first false healer charged a fortune for his services. My dear, as you contemplate your future, please do not confuse the work that you will do to earn a living with this subject that we are communicating about!

The baker and the cleaning lady that I told you about were both in great demand, and in this sense, their lot was improved by how they went about their work. In my own doctoring, I am sure that a part of my success has to do with this very thing. But not the baker, the cleaning lady, nor I attach a price or, as the business people say, a "premium" to our work; it is simply that this is how we choose to work.

This work is meant for heaven and comes from heaven; charging for it would be like charging for love! And if you ever wish to see what results in the souls of those who turn love into a transaction, simply study the eyes and the countenances of those who do.

The second false healer I will tell you about worked as a masseuse. For most, her work was memorable chiefly because her clients came to know so much about her colorful personal life. But clients who were particularly sensitive developed strange afflictions after her sessions: headaches, indigestion, inflammation in their joints, nightmares, insomnia, and disturbing patterns of thought.

It was her habit to treat each client as if they were a close confidant, and while she worked, she freely shared with each of them the goings on of her failing relationships, her violent boyfriends, and frequent encounters with the police. She actively sought advice from her clients, some of whom were more than happy to give it, but she never took it seriously as she had no wish to change. Yet for those who were particularly sensitive, all of this unasked-for input coupled with their own wish for a relaxing massage created a mixed message that could then take their souls days or weeks to reconcile.

In truth, the message was not at all mixed, as the rhythms and intensity of the massage strokes followed perfectly the storylines of this false healer. Fast, heavy strokes when she was telling about her anger; hard, twisting strokes when she was describing her emotions as she tried to hold on to a relationship with a man with uncontrolled moods. But the results in her sensitive clients were always the same: Instead of coming away from her massage relaxed and rejuvenated, they came away bruised and exhausted.

This false healer held a wish for all to be involved in the drama of her life and to extend to her their sympathy. And in this way, she avoided any quiet work that could have opened her to see her life objectively. So beware of this second type of false healer, whose soul harbors a spirit resistant to self-examination.

With every type of false healer, there will be some kind of mixed message. Words may not be in accord with actions, such as body language, posture, and facial expressions. And the habits of the eyes will tell a different story compared to the words a false healer uses. So it must become a skill and then a habit to sense mixed messages of all types.

The third type of false healer is the most destructive—a wolf in sheep's clothing! While the arrogance and laziness of the first two types have hurtful results, there is nothing personal in the fallout from their work—the affected clients could be anyone. But the third type has a soul that harbors a predatory spirit that is deeply personal.

For the first two types of false healers, the poison of arrogance is easy to spot. It is never covered by more than the thinnest mask of reasonableness. A soul poisoned by a lazy spirit makes them care not at all to obscure their true motives. They are there, out in the open, for all to see. But the third false healer is cut from different cloth. They may work in a hospital, school, or religious institution, always in some helpful capacity. They can work in any walk of life that puts them in contact with vulnerable people who must share with them personal, even intimate, details of their lives.

These false healers prowl for these details as pickpockets spy out hidden wallets, but it is not the feeding upon these details that fills their bellies. Their main sustenance comes from finding how these details leave

vulnerabilities in the psyches of their clients. Vulnerabilities that, like a key in the hand of a thief, give them
entry at a time of their own choosing to feast on the
finer energies of a soul. We will leave for another time
this subject of the finer energies of the soul, as we will
need to cover it in detail. But for now, beware this
third type of false healer, whose soul harbors the spirit
of a predator, one whose wish is to hunt and feast on
the pure, the weak, and the innocent!

I remember one of these who was a nurse, and her
hospital job was puncturing veins and drawing blood.
She met many afflicted people and earned their trust by
the skill of her painless needling. One of her patients
was a young man who was shy and lonely, owing to a
speech impediment that was, to him, a deep source of
shame. She befriended him, and he instantly became
dependent on her attentions, which she dispensed to
him as with a tiny eyedropper.

She played with him—she would promise to meet
him and not show up or meet him but then only speak
with others and talk about him as if he weren't there. I
was present at one occasion and happened to observe
her methods. It was as if within the predatory spirit in
her soul, there were other spirits that, like tools within

a toolbox, surfaced when needed. When she wanted his attention, she spoke to him in a seductive tone, but by the end of her words, her tone changed to a taunt. When she corrected his speech, she began to speak in a helpful tone, but by the end of her words, her tone changed to be patronizing. And when he expressed a wish, she used words that sounded agreeable, but her tone was full of contempt.

I have always been fascinated with how the tones of speech color its meaning. And it seems to me they perfectly reflect a spirit within a soul that, for the moment, happens to show itself. For the most part, this young man was blind to her deceptions, but on this one occasion, I saw that he suspected that she was being insincere with him. Yet, she was highly attuned to this, and she was skillful enough to seamlessly suppress these spirits and dial back her tone to cover her deceptions until his suspicion had passed.

By only pretending to care, it cost her nothing, and for years she was able to keep him thinking about and pining for her without end. It was on this energy that she feasted. Her behavior reminded me of what my tropical diseases professor taught me in school: Some organisms are considered perfect parasites, because they cleverly lull their hosts into believing that they are not infested.

Any realm amenable to bringing in a spirit of healing can even more easily serve as a conduit for its opposite, so it is easy for any of these spirits to affect your work. Not as much as it did with these three I've mentioned, but in little ways—as a drop of ink leaves a gallon of pure water looking faintly grey. A tinge of arrogance in a sea of compassion creates a bit of impatience, a tinge of laziness in a sea of diligence creates missed chances to discover the heart of a matter, and a tinge of predation in an otherwise charitable sea turns a feeling of trust into a question of trust. Everything depends upon intent, strength of awareness, and integrity to be in accord with the highest kind of love.

But you may be asking how to clean house and rid it of these ignoble traces? That is a big subject, and if you are interested, just let me know; we can cover it at another time.

I want to leave you with one final thought, my dear: All false healers practice as they do out of a profound lack of any sense that they can be fed from above. And while there can be an honest sense of this in those who are humbled by their own inner state, in false healers, this sense arises instead out of a fear of never getting all of what they feel they need. Those who are insecure without humbleness, those who are arrogant, or those who have no belief in what can come from above will always be difficult to heal, but when they hold themselves out as helpers to the ill or weak, they gravely harm others even as they further their own disconnection.

Your loving uncle,

James

On Faith & Reason

My Dearest Madeline,

It was good to hear back from you so soon, but your questions about cleaning house must wait until my next letter, as I surely understand your wish to know what came between your father and me. But to understand that rift, you first need to learn something essential about the times in which we live.

Remember what I told you about how harboring an arrogant spirit or a fearful insecurity closes the window to heaven? And how, with that channel closed, there is no chance of bringing the energies of heaven into one's life? There is one other thing that can close off this channel, something that can mimic arrogance and merge into arrogance but is itself not arrogant. It is a belief that heaven cannot exist, because science cannot measure it. And if the god of science is a yardstick, then there can be no God beyond mass superstition, no consciousness beyond thoughts in a brain, and no love beyond hormones that assure survival. So then there can be no soul, no world of spirits, no survival of anything following death, and no sense of any profound connection between all people and among all living things. Each person then with their cloistered brain is considered complete, independent, and autonomous; the sense of heaven and a window to heaven are simply considered absurd.

And while these beliefs seem to cause little harm to scientists themselves, they have a real effect on practices such as medicine, where doctors are educated to believe that truth cannot exist unless it is measurable in an obvious way.

I think that had your father and I been drawn to sports or art as children, we could have remained close, but he and I were drawn to medicine. Our temperaments were different. He was more the engineer and a gifted mechanic, and I was more of a philosopher. His interest led him to surgery, and mine led me to what is called *palliative care*—when a person near the end of their life can no longer be cured of their ills, but doctoring can still help them have a good quality of life in their remaining days.

Your father and I had a patient in common, a man named Thomas. Your father had done a difficult surgery on Thomas that did not go well, and I was the one who took care of Thomas in his final days. Your father had done all that he could. It was just that Thomas' body was too weak to recover. Your father had a personal stake in him, as he had been his favorite teacher in medical school. But your father was deeply offended when he learned of how I had taken care of him.

Your father, Thomas, and most of the elders of our society hold the belief, whether they realize it or not, that if something cannot be measured, then it cannot exist. This principle arose in science hundreds of years ago and divided science away from religion. All at once, there were laws that described the movements of the stars and the idea that laws of nature could predict these things created a belief that, in time, everything could be known.

And the mysteries of heaven became quaint in

their eyes. And, in truth, this was a needed rift, as the Church had grown political and wished to control all knowledge, even knowledge far beyond what its teachings were capable of explaining. But despite this needed change, there was a cost to this split. It caused learned men to dismiss the sense that insubstantial things—God, Love, Consciousness—exist as more than just ideas or chemical secretions.

And with the window to heaven closed, the ideas in these men's heads grew in intensity as does boiling water when heated in a pressure pot. The rumble of these ideas, boiling without vent, drowned out the fainter, subtler sounds that murmur in the heart, sounds that, in a more balanced soul, temper the intellect with kindness and wisdom. And science thus fell into the same error that plagued religion: It wished to control all knowledge, even knowledge far beyond what its teachings were capable of explaining.

As the field of medicine grew, it took on this core belief, and the world was seen as a grand mechanism. And the human body was seen this way as well. And to this day, doctors are educated to understand the body strictly from this perspective. To one so trained, there can be no God, no soul, no spirit life, nothing except ideas in a brain that cease at death. And the window to heaven that permits the communion so central to healing is sealed shut, not by a spirit of arrogance or a fearful insecurity but by beliefs that shun the idea that heaven even exists.

In your father's field of surgery, his beliefs made little difference, as surgical work focuses on the most mechanical aspects of a sick or injured body. But his beliefs got in our way when I assumed the care of this man, whom your father held in the highest esteem.

Thomas was an elder in our society and held on to these same beliefs your father did, and I had no interest in trying to change him. I had been down this road before and knew better than to confront a patient with their own ideas about mortality if they harbored an unshakable opinion that all would end for them at the moment of death. Thomas felt this way, and all he needed from me was caring to ease his suffering.

But near the end of his life, he had some experiences that he could not explain and could not dismiss. On his last day, in a moment of clarity, he whispered a question into my ear. "Please," he said, "Please tell me . . . are you going bald on the top of your head?" What a strange question! You see, I am tall, and I had always only seen him when he was in bed, so there was no way that he could ever see the top of my head. He seemed desperate to know this trivial fact, but I thought better than asking him why this was important to him, as it seemed to take so much of his strength to get his question out—I didn't want him to lose any more strength in having to explain himself.

So, I told him that yes, I was, and I bent way over so that he could see the top of my head. He then said, "I saw that bald spot from up by the ceiling—I was up there while still in this bed. It must have been a dream! But it couldn't have been a dream, because I saw your bald spot *exactly* as I see it now . . . so it couldn't have been a dream. It must have really happened." And with that, he became agitated.

I felt obliged to share with him, as gently as I could, that there was good science behind what are called *out of body experiences*, and, like him, many have seen things that could not be the hallucinations of a failing brain but that must, instead, be the result of an aspect of awareness that exists independent of our body. It appeared that he was ready to argue with me . . . that he had defended his worldview on this subject to students for decades, and it seemed that my comments had triggered the start of his much-used argument. But he stopped himself, sat up, and said, "But I *saw* your bald spot!" And then he died.

When your father learned of this episode, he accused me of preaching and trying to convert a dying man. I told him that I was only trying to comfort him in his agitation, and besides, I had no religious affiliation to convert him into. But he grew angry with me and said that he would never refer a patient to me again.

I knew that this rift had been a long time coming, as your father felt threatened by the prospect of there being any kind of awareness outside of the brain. To him, my belief in the workings of the soul and the spirits it contains, the nature of healing, and, of course, the way in which a charm carved by your Simon could heal a damaged soul were all superstition, charlatanism, muddled thinking, and the like. I knew he would not speak to me again and that he would shield you and your brother from my influence. But there was nothing I could do. I tried to see him as he lay dying, but he was clear in his instructions that he did not wish to see me.

Here is a good time to ponder something for

your future: Know that there can be no greater, further-reaching healing—not dealing with poverty, war, disease, or ignorance—than if even just a single person can be brought into an experience that wakens them to their own window to heaven. Only then can the steam of their jumbled thoughts escape upward and the murmurs of their heart begin to temper their experiences in ways great and small—that will change their way of being in our world. And if possible, on a second level, they will come to understand that knowing in their heart is not at all the same as a belief in an idea, any more than the experience of a sunrise relates to knowing the measured distance to the sun. And if possible, on a third and still deeper level, they will catch a glimpse in their heart of the connectedness of all living things, not as a concept but as a lived experience—where their own connection, streaming from above, is felt to be just one of the countless rays from the common source of which we are all a part.

Fostering that kind of healing is only possible when there is a relationship in place that is built on trust, when there is a spirit of compassion securely in place, and when the strength of your presence carries with it the sense that you understand that which is most needed. Then, at a time, a place, and a circumstance chosen only by heaven, it is possible to bring a glimpse of heaven deeply into someone's experience—something real that they will not be able to explain or dismiss. Simon, of course, was a master of this, but so was your mother, who kissed your knee and got you to stop crying.

So, there you have it my dear; now you know. But also know that your father was an excellent surgeon. He was not known for his bedside manner, but when there was a need for a complicated and difficult surgery, he was known as the best, and you have every right to be proud of him, as I am.

Your loving uncle,

James

On Souls & Spirits

My Dearest Madeline,

Thank you for your kind words. It was difficult to share with you the rift that stood between your father and me, not so much because of any wrong that I felt guilty of, but because I did not, in any way, wish for you to find in my heart any disparagement toward him. There was none, and there is none—far from it. I always have and always will hold him in my highest regard. But loyalties within a family can play strange tricks on the meaning of words and can conflate intentions beyond any semblance of the truth. So I thank you for acknowledging this; I didn't want a misconception to stand between us in this regard.

So now we come to your question of how to clean house, and I had to laugh when you relayed to me that story of how Simon would scrub out his chimney every night.[12] I can tell you for certain that he performed that ritual only for your benefit. Had you not been there, he wouldn't have troubled himself with such a task. But that was part of his mastery—he knew that this act would leave a deep impression in you, and so it has.

There are many parts to the answer of what you ask, but knowing you as I do, I can be certain of at least where you will need to begin. But first, I must tell you this story.

Years ago, I was visiting a school of martial arts located in the hills on the way up to Moon Lake.[13] On the day that I arrived, I witnessed the strangest sporting event that I had ever seen. There were seven young students, all of similar height, who were taking part in a competition. The arena for this competition

---

12   *The Charm Carver*, p 81.
13   Ibid., p 67.

was a natural pool of water that was deep enough so that no one standing on the bottom would have their head above the water line. But affixed to the bottom of this pool was a single, narrow pedestal with a platform on its top that was wide enough for just one person to stand on. The height of the pedestal allowed any of these students to stand upright and have their entire head, but only their head, protrude above the water.

Each student was given a phrase of twenty-one words that they had to memorize; that was the easy part. They then all entered the pool, and each had to try to stand on the pedestal and recite their twenty-one-word phrase to completion, while below the surface all the other contestants were swimming hard, battering the standing one, while each of them attempted to mount the pedestal for their own recital.

As you might imagine, this was a difficult competition. But I stood by and made a note of the fragments that I heard from each young student. In the course of half an hour each one of them had mounted the pedestal several times and gotten off just a bit of their phrase. Here is what I heard:

1. "I'm cold, I'm tired, and I don't like this
   game one bit . . ."

2. "There's a new girl in school, and I'd sure like
   to meet her . . ."

3. "Nobody better try to push me off of this
   pedestal . . ."

4. "I can't wait for lunch today. They're making
   my favorite . . ."

5. "If I wrap my toes around this platform, I can
   hold on long enough to . . ."

6. "If only I'd learned from a young age to swim,
   I'd not be in this pickle I'm in . . ."

7. "Six times seven is forty-two; six times eight
   is forty-eight . . ."

In the end, all of the students were exhausted, and not one could finish their whole twenty-one-word phrase before being pushed off the platform and replaced by another.

I asked the master about this competition. It seemed so pointless. I couldn't imagine anyone winning as long as there was at least one other contestant still strong enough to topple the one standing. He told me that winning was not the point. But what he then told me relates to this question that you have pressed me to answer.

If you are to clean house, the first thing you must do is see what needs cleaning. Then you need to learn what can be cleaned and how and what will need to be thrown out and how. And then you must see what you must learn to live with, because it cannot be cleaned, and it cannot be thrown away. Your first task is to observe what is going on inside. And as you do, you will soon see that your inner world is not much different than this sporting event that I have just told you about.

You will find a chorus of voices, each with something to say—a stream of thought, an urge, a desire, a fear or an anxiety, maybe a song, maybe a love—all rising up to your awareness, only to be displaced by another after only a moment or just a fraction of a moment.

You must see what is going on without any attempt to change what you find, because inner observing, at its lowest level, is nothing more than vanity; there is judgment and comparison to others. But on the next higher level of inner observing, there is no judgment—just seeing what is true. It is in the nature of our consciousness that we can view things from different levels, and in this kind of observation, there are many levels above the ones that I have just described. But for now, don't concern yourself with those; focus only on seeing the stream of activity in your mind moment by moment.

It is best not to tinker with the machine until you learn how it works! You must first learn what tools there are to clean with and how to use them. You may feel that these voices are just patterns of your thoughts, and so by simple strength of will, you will be able to quiet them. But my dear, nothing could be further from the truth! If you subscribe to the beliefs of the elders, then this is the way you will look at things. But as I have already told you, our world is not so simple.

Each pattern of thought, each urge, each feeling is a pairing of our human form with a particular spirit that gains a bit of life by flowing through us. And spirits, as a rule, are hungry for this experience and will swim hard to stay in the game and to gain the upper hand. These spirits are attracted to our soul, which itself is a kind of vessel, by a kind of resonance—like a choir-master's pitch pipe holding her choir to a particular key but also like a magnet attracting a piece of iron. Scientists are beginning to guess where these pairings occur—where parts of atoms, spinning in clouds, synchronize from randomness and spin together like a room full of dervishes!

The attraction can be through inheritance—like the broad spirits that hold the patterns of the human form that are particular to geography or culture or the narrow spirits that hold the shapes of noses and ears among members of the same family. These spirits pair with our genetics and are mostly fixed, but, with the right kind of efforts, some can change.

The attraction can be by possession—a common occurrence in everyone's soul—like a spirit of anger or a spirit of passion overtaking our experiences. These spirits pair with our emotions and can be altered through a kind of inner struggle. And while religions often call this *spiritual warfare*, and it can feel like a battle to curate and tame the spirits that are not harmonious with our chosen nature, after a time, these more invasive spirits can become less our enemies than our allies. For what champion can ever grow in speed, strength, or skill without challenges from worthy opponents?

Or the attraction can be curated by choice, like spirits that contain entire bodies of knowledge, such as music, mathematics, language, sports, or any craft that has a long and storied history. These spirits are invited in through diligent study and apprenticeship so that one who masters a field becomes a living embodiment of that spirit.

It is a misunderstanding that our spirit and our soul are the same thing; they are made of different stuff. And all these spirits that live through us and our spirit—though we use the same word—are as different as a thread is to a tapestry. This is a big subject, and if you are interested, we can cover it at another time. But for now, try to appreciate that your experience is only partly you. To believe otherwise is akin to an open window believing itself to be the breeze blowing through it.

Let me tell you a story about a patient of mine who I took care of near the end of her life.

In her early years, Lorraine lived in a home ruled by her tyrannical father. Back then, before she had the awareness or the strength to curate spirits of her own choosing, a spirit of oppression was implanted deeply within her. This spirit resonated with other spirits throughout her soul, but I will only tell you of the ones that relate to my care of her, namely those on her periphery—the ones that pair with the body's structure—such as those carrying the patterns of her stature.

She grew without the three forward curves of her spine: the lower one that makes space in the belly for food and for vitality, the middle one that makes room in the chest for air and for the emotions of the heart, and the upper one that curates our experience and our expressiveness. And without these curves, her back was shaped more like a turtle's than like a willow branch, and so she had suffered all of her life with problems of digestion, breathing, and speech.

I have always been fascinated by how different curves of the spine, postures of the head, and expressions of the face together seem to attract certain spirits and their attendant attributes. It is as if the spine and the head form an antenna, and bending them this way and that tune one's entire experience.

For example, posturing the head way in front of the spine and furrowing one's brow attracts an intellectual spirit that is cut off from the emotions of the heart; constricting the middle and lower spine while tilting the head backward attracts a spirit of grieving; while exaggerating the forward curve of the lower spine, constricting the middle spine, and jutting the chin attracts a spirit of arrogance, and so on.

The oppressive spirit within Lorraine resonated with spirits up and down her spine. The one tuned to her upper spine gave her voice a high and thin tone that lacked any depth of color. The one tuned to her middle spine made it all but impossible for her heart to recognize genuine love, even when it came her way. And the one that tuned to her lower spine was one that I have written to you about before—a spirit of fearful insecurity that blinded her of her window to heaven.

When she became my patient, she was nearing the end of her life, but she had a real wish to be rid of these spirits that had fouled her soul. In truth, any of her manifestations could have been a point of entry to upright her ship—they could each have been used as a lever, connected as they were through their shared resonances with all the spirits singing round the core of her oppression. And if she had been stronger, we would have had the luxury of finding which of these would have had the greatest effect.

In people in less dire straits, the linkages between their core and their periphery are weak, and so correcting one can have no bearing on any of the others.

So it can be a long process identifying each manifestation and freeing the body from them. But in her state, though she wasn't strong, her wish, her inner wish,[14] was as strong as it could be.

I have seen this often in my work with those near the ends of their lives and in those who have learned this secret of the dying—they don't have time to waste, and they live more fully than most of us do when the shadow of death is not pressing in so hard. And in a circumstance like hers, the inner wish strengthens the links among and between these various spirits, so any lever gains the capacity to do the whole job. A strong inner wish is a powerful thing indeed!

I got her to sit up as straight as she could, drop her shoulders, erect her head, broaden her chest, and then simply breathe, slowly and deeply—inflating her belly as she did. I told her to pay no attention to any thoughts or feelings that seemed to come through her but to focus again and again on her posture and breathing, as a lifetime of bad habits—in the posture of her spine, in the set of her muscles, and in the spirits—had crystallized into rigid patterns within her

---

14   *The Charm Carver*, p 59.

soul. This would require her to catch herself, again and again, as she fell back into her old manifestations.

I told her that the most important thing was for her not to judge her falling back as a failure or as an act deserving of embarrassment, contempt, or grief, because this kind of occurrence is as foundational to our spirit life as gravity is to our physical life. Rather, she needed to cultivate a spirit of patience and steadfastness and to feel only compassion toward herself.

After three days of diligence and following vents of anger, grief, and tears, there came a light to her eyes and a loss of the lines on her face, and the tone of her voice developed a depth that she herself had never heard before. And she told me that a spirit of peace had finally entered her, and she was glad she had lived to experience this.

So, my dear niece, start with observation. See if you can train your awareness to see from the point of view that the martial arts master and I had while we were standing at the side of the pool, watching the competition. I look forward to hearing from you.

Your loving uncle,
James

On a Compassionate Heart

My Dearest Madeline,

Again, you are fretful! But this time, I have had a hand in this! The task I gave you was far tougher than you expected. But before I explain what made it so, I will tell you this story.

There is a mountain not far from where your father and I were born. Our family lived in the town by its base. Growing up in the shadow of a mountain is a humbling thing; just gazing at its splendor took your breath away. And yet, few of my friends ever climbed the mountain, but your dad and I did. To do so, we had to train—our legs had to be made strong, we had to learn the map that showed the way up, and we had to learn to raise our threshold of frustration, because as we started climbing, we got lost, and we fell down a lot!

We were lucky that an old man in town knew about climbing, and he told us to not completely trust the map. "The map is not the territory," he said. He also told us that the most important muscles to develop were the ones that would sense when we were about to fall. "In time," he said, "these muscles will catch you even before you slip." I asked him how we could strengthen these muscles quickly, and he laughed and said, "Gravity is a great teacher—you have to fall down a lot!"

After months of training, we climbed and saw the view from the top. It was more magnificent than anything we could imagine. The day we got back, your father and I were so excited by what we had seen, and we told everyone. And in our zeal, we believed that once we shared our experience with our friends, they would want to see this for themselves. We even offered to help them train, as by then we knew how to do it. But we were mistaken. None of our friends ever took us up on our offer. They were entertained by our adventure, but they were content and didn't wish to exert themselves for the sake of a grander view.

In your letter, you told me that you couldn't observe your inner streams of thoughts and feelings in real time, as if from the outside, looking in. But only upon reflection—after the fact—could you see that your attention had been pulled this way and that by forces swimming within your soul, each gaining a brief upper hand. I've described to you how this appears from a higher perspective. But without the strength needed to obtain this view, you are left seeing your experience only from the inside, looking out. If I may, I'd like to put words to that experience, so that later, you will understand much.

Imagine a fast-moving river, the kind that people raft on for the thrill of the whitewater. But unlike a conventional river, this one forks frequently into sidestreams, some of which reconnect with the first river farther downstream; others connect into other fast-moving rivers nearby, each of which also fork frequently.

Imagine that you are in this river, but you have no raft; you can't swim well. You can float if the current isn't too rough, but if it is, you struggle not to drown.

You may end up carried down the main river, or at any point, the current may pull you into any sidestream and then into any other river. You never really know what route you will end up taking because you are being *taken*. You are pulled along by these currents and have no idea where you will land.

This is a picture of our common experience. Outside of brief spasms when we manage to swim a few strokes and land in a particular stream, our attention is held by one spirit and then another, and each, like a current, captures us and off we go.

These spirits each gain a bit of life in the moments when we reside in their flow. We become a part of them, and they live through us. Imagine any time that you have felt angry. In that moment, a spirit of anger flows through you, and it can feel like something foreign to your nature. You may feel a surge of energy in that anger, but when the moment passes, you may notice that you feel depleted. This spirit gained a bit of life, and it came at your expense.

Spirits live off our attention as we live off of food.[15] And frightening as it may sound, in moments

---

15   *The Charm Carver*, p 78.

like these, we are being *consumed* in tiny, little bites. This is the nature of spiritual existence: We must pay, whether we like it or not, to be carried by the flow of any spirit. And, in the world of spirit, we humans are mostly like sheep; we are tended to and nibbled at—not physically but spiritually, as our attention is a delight to them.

Yet we can benefit from the forces of these currents. But to do so, we must be able to choose among them and not simply be carried along. And for this, we must be strong enough to swim at least with our heads above the water. With more strength, we can swim to the shore and stand apart, like the martial arts instructor and I did, and view the currents from the outside looking in. With yet more strength, we can construct a raft with oar and rudder and navigate between and among the streams and not risk drowning, even in the roughest water.

Then it will be like the difference between having your pocket picked or opening your purse and making a purchase. But to make this a choice, you must see that these little thefts are happening and not just after the fact. In time, it will be possible for you to curate your soul, making it into a raft with oar and rudder and by this means choosing the spirits—the streams and rivers—that shape the course of your life.

Now seems as good a time as any to enter the subject of healing. But to grasp what healing is, you must first have a sense of what life is. This is another big subject, but for now, I'll confine myself to a simple question: What is the difference between a lump of coal, a diamond, a toasted scone, and a human heart?

Coal is made of carbon. A diamond is made of carbon. The toasted parts of a scone are made of carbon, and the cells of a human heart contain an abundance of carbon. So what's the difference between the carbon in the coal, the diamond, the scone, and the heart?

The elders will tell you that there is no difference. "Carbon is carbon," they would say. But the pairing of form with spirit is not confined to humans. There is a kind of life in everything that advances in steps from lowest to highest. The lowest forms pair just with spirits of structure—coal holds just this kind of spirit.

I've already told you that spirits swim and swim hard, and once they pair with us, they feel to us like a current, as their swimming flows through us. From their perspective, they vie for our attention, and once they pair with our form, they flow through us. But from our perspective, we only notice that we are being carried. The world of spirit is, indeed, very strange! But, there is more. The pairing itself is a kind of song and dance. There has to be a kind of resonance, like form and spirit each singing the same song, to bring a particular form together to dance with a particular spirit. For example, the form of a diamond is more organized and regular than the form of coal, and the spirit of a diamond sings a purer note and dances a more synchronized dance than does the spirit of coal.

The carbon in the scone holds spirit on more levels than does the carbon in coal or diamond. Among others, it holds the structural spirit of the dough and the spirits of the plant kingdom and the spirit of wheat. The carbon in the heart holds yet additional levels of spirit. Among many, it holds the structural spirit of heart muscles, the spirits of the kingdoms of animals and of humans, the spirit of its particular human, and under certain circumstances, it may hold higher spirits of perception—such as beauty, truth, and love.

Not beauty in the usual sense, but beauty as would be seen through the eyes of God, such as acts of kindness and undeserved generosity; not truth in the usual sense, but truth with the ring of wisdom and genuine moral authority; and not love in the usual sense, but selfless love, or what is called *love without possession*.

In these higher spirits of perception, the feeling that gives a sense of beauty, truth, and love is a resonance that there is beauty on all levels, truth on all levels, and love on all levels. This is different from our common perception, where we may see beauty on one level but be blind to a countering sense of vulgarity, for example, on another level. It is similar for truth and love.

Higher perception notices mixed messages and the dissonances they cause. So when all levels resonate in accord, there is a feeling of complete beauty, complete truth, and complete love. In fact, the whole sense of real completeness is held in the realm of these higher spirits of perception.

Remember the cleaning lady that I told you about? She sensed that her work was complete when all of her perceptions registered this, and she felt this in her heart. Simon once told me that he knew that his carving of a charm was done when he had a feeling in his heart that told him, "Yes, it is done." And perhaps you know of the Lord of all Christians, whose last words, uttered as were all of his words, from a source within his heart: "It is finished."

If all of your levels can sing in accord, you will attract these higher spirits. But without your own levels harmonized first, you won't perceive if there is harmony among the levels of anything else.

And something more, my dearest niece: There is the possibility that a heart made ready to hold these higher spirits may hold a spirit of healing; as when this spirit is welcome in a soul, this is where it resides.

The pairing of all these levels of spirit takes place in the inner structure of carbon, but carbon is just an example. I could have chosen hydrogen, but that would have led us into the subject of homeopathy, and this is a big subject as it is.

Scientists know that groups of atoms, atoms themselves, parts of atoms, and parts of parts of atoms each possess clouds that spin and orbit in unknowable ways. In the levels of these clouds, spirit pairs with form through a kind of singing and dancing, adding synchronizations to the spins and orbits within these unknowable clouds. Spirit swims hard to pair with form, and then form flows along in the river of spirit. It is all a dance, my dear.

The carbon of diamond contains a cloud where the dancing is more synchronized than the carbon of coal. To the spirit world, the carbon in the scone is like a dance hall of many levels, each dancing to a different song. And the carbon in the human heart has clouds with dancing on even more levels.

But here there is this additional chance: that the dancing on each level can be brought to the same song, and in this more synchronized environment, the soul then attracts these finer energies. In the case of the human heart, these can be the higher spirits of perception—beauty, truth, and love—that only come when there is this greater synchronization. The spirits on all levels must be in accord, singing in harmony and dancing together like a room full of dervishes.

This is how compassion grows, and this is what a spirit of healing needs for it to make a home within a heart. When you meet someone who contains this inner harmony you will sense a presence about them—a feeling of integrity, kindness, patience, and openness. Ah! Like your old friend Simon!

And though healing is a big subject, there isn't much to explain—it's really very simple. But, as your father and I learned, the map is not the territory.

Healing itself is on different levels: the skin on your bruised knee, an illness, your hurt pride, the anguish of grieving. In each, a pattern of song and dance is disturbed, where parts of atoms, spinning in clouds, lose their finer synchronizations and revert to the greater randomness found in more lifeless matter. Healing starts with bringing back harmony from where it has been disturbed.

The cells of skin all sing a tone like members in a choir, and a bruise is a clashing note. The music is not of our world; we can't hear it, but maybe we can sense it. Healing begins when a choir-master of some kind sounds a note and brings the cells back into harmony. This sets the tone for the whole healing process.

It is the same with illness, but the music is more song than note, with liver and spleen singing vitality and illness sounding a clashing melody. Here a choir-master sounds not a note but great chords, and the organs begin their path back to harmony.

It is the same with afflictions of the mind and of the heart: Only here, the choir-master must sound entire songs, entire symphonies—to harmonize the more complex dissonances that arise on these levels.

If the cells or organs have enough vitality, a choir-master rises from their own ranks, but if not, help can come from the outside from someone who has harmonized their own vitality and stored enough of it to share.

If the mind or the heart is well harmonized, a choir-master rises from their own ranks. But if not, help must come from a source that can intervene with corresponding complexity. What is called for is some-one who, in addition to having harmonized her own vitality and stored enough to share, has also so curated the spirits within her soul so that a spirit of healing, a facet of the love of God, can flow through her. And while the energy of vitality can be stored and shared, like water from a dammed-up stream, a spirit of heal-ing is like a breeze—it cannot be stored; it must be received, blowing in through a window from heaven, and shared within the moment.

It is worth mentioning that healing always has these two sources that aid the vitality of the one in need of healing: one's own stored, excess vitality and the spirit of healing that comes down from God. In bringing healing to a simple bruise, it can be almost entirely the former, but in bringing healing to a soul, it will be almost entirely the latter—with one's excess vitality here only useful, like Simon cleaning his chim-ney, to keep the channel open and clean.

It is also worth mentioning that what flows *through* us and what comes *from* us relates to our spirit and our soul. Our spirit is a thousand rivers that all belong to God, and like drops of water in a flow, all revert back to Him when we die. Without a trace of our awareness or individuality remaining, our life experiences just barely alter the flavor of these waters. But what we do in life with our spirit can cultivate our soul, and it can become our raft—a sturdy vessel that can then ferry our awareness beyond the reaches of time.

Who can be a choir-master? Someone who can hold a pure tone in the face of dissonance or even chaos. This is why it is important to practice compassion without sympathy, like the police officer that I told you about. You must be sensitive to a person's suffering but grounded enough so that you are not consumed by the same spirits that feast on this person.

You'll need a raft to float above and navigate among these churning spirits; otherwise, you'll end up carried down the same streams as this person is. To build your raft, you'll need to see what is dissonant or chaotic within yourself and, when you have sufficient vitality, clean these things up. That is why I had you begin to look inside, but you need to get stronger before you'll be able to see more objectively, let alone build your own raft. Consciousness is like this—with greater levels of vitality, you will be able to shift your perspective and see among more and more levels of spirit.

To strengthen your vitality, you'll need to build up three spiritual muscles: the muscle of attention that enables you to focus on a particular thing without distraction, the muscle of awareness that enables you to finely sense your interior and exterior environments without comment, and the muscle of intent that allows you to make deliberate choices. And you'll need to stop losing vitality through habits that drain it away. This will help you accumulate vitality beyond your basic needs.

With added strength, you'll begin to swim within the currents of spirit and not just be *taken* by them. Eventually, you will be able swim to the shore and stand, high and dry, and see the currents that vie for your attention. This, like the view from the mountaintop, will give you a perspective that for now, as you discovered, you can only imagine.

Your greatest hindrances will come from the spirits that, uninvited, feast on your attention and the habits that drain you. The subject of habits is a big one, and if you are interested, we can cover it at another time. But in terms of these uninvited spirits, at first, it is not a matter of trying to resist them, as they all swim hard, and right now, you can barely keep your head above the water. Rather you must cultivate an awareness that is parallel to what is going on in your mind, but is in your body.

Set aside time every day to focus all of your attention just on some sensation of your body. It can be as simple as sitting in good posture in a straight-back chair with your hands folded in your lap and finding a position that you can hold in absolute stillness except for the motions of your breathing. Then focus just on the sensations of the air entering and leaving your nose; listen to the faint sounds of the air as it moves, and feel your chest and belly fill and empty.

Thoughts will come, feelings will come, urges will come; ignore them—focus only on these sensations. If you are drawn in by a thought stream, eventually you will catch yourself and bring yourself back to your sensation. Above all, don't judge yourself for falling back into your thoughts; it does not mean that you are a failure, and don't feel embarrassed or fretful, as this kind of falling is as foundational to our spirit life as falling from gravity is to our physical life.

You must raise your threshold of frustration. Just as your father and I strengthened our muscles before we could climb the mountain, it is in this process of catching yourself falling into your thought stream and bringing yourself back to your sensation, again and again and again, that will build the kinds of muscles that will help you with everything else. And as you go about this, cultivate a spirit of patience and steadfastness, and feel only compassion toward yourself.

With diligent practice and over a long period of time, you will be able to switch at will between having your attention be just within your sensation and having it be within your thought stream, regardless of how compelling or urgent the pull happens to be.

When you get to the point where you can, as it were, stand on the shore and watch your thought stream flow like a river and choose whether or not to put your toe in the water, you will have accumulated sufficient attention, awareness, and intent to begin curating the spirits in your soul, banishing those that obscure your window to heaven and choosing those you wish to keep. Doing this, you will feel a blossoming sense of integrity and, with it, the compassion that is so central to a spirit of healing.

There are many exercises besides this focusing on breathing, but it is best not to fill your mind now with a catalog of them all! But for variety's sake, here are two more. Walk without thought—no words in your head. Anchor your awareness on the sensations of your weight rolling across the soles of your feet and the ever-changing sounds of your footfalls while taking in all the sights, sounds, smells, and sensations that enter your perception. This is best done in natural surroundings, but I have also done this walking city streets. The challenge is that your senses are taking in impressions, and you must find your own way to take this all in, without being *taken* by any of it.

Lastly, in another quiet, sitting exercise, follow the sensation of your heart beating, and move your awareness to the sensations of blood pulsing to your extremities. See if you can sense the pulse of this flow in the soles of your feet and in your hands and fingers.

In the beginning, these exercises will feel like chores, and you will have to make time to do them. But I learned this from Simon—that if carrying a spirit of healing becomes important to you, you will make exercises out of all parts of your life, and in each moment, you will be practicing something. It will then not feel like a chore, as tending to the spirits in your soul will become for you like cultivating a beautiful garden, and this will become a central current of your inner life.

In all of these exercises, practice this: Take your attention out of your mind, put it into your body, and hold it there with a spirit of contemplation. This will strengthen your attention, your awareness, and your intent, and they will all grow in length, width, and depth!

Let me know how it goes!

Your loving uncle,
James

On Vitality

My Dearest Madeline,

I am so pleased to learn of your working in a plant nursery. Bringing a healing spirit to plants is a wonderful thing, as they are so responsive and never ask for much. I'll have more to say about that, but first let me address the part in your letter where you told me that many things are getting in your way—hindrances, obstacles—all kinds of things that interfere with your earnest intentions. These seem to be circling around something that is not at all clear to me; maybe it is clear to you? If you know what it is, don't be shy about sharing it with me in your next letter.

I have no doubt that some of what troubles you comes from the spirits that carry you where they may. And so it may seem like a riddle with no answer, because if these interferences keep you from building the strength you need to deal with them, how will you ever be able to clean house?

The exercises that build your spiritual muscles also create different qualities of energy that get stored in something like a series of spiritual buckets. Your vitality is a measure of how full these buckets become. But now we need to speak not so much of the ways to add to your buckets but of other things—things that touch on all of what troubles you now. You see, it's hard for any of these buckets to fill if there are holes in them, because any fuel you manage to add just leaks out, without a trace of any gain for you.

So, I will mostly confine myself to the things that poke holes in your buckets. These are all the things that drain away vitality and so make it hard to do anything new, anything that has not already become a habit. Because once your body has mastered a task, it requires little attention, and so the precious energy of attention is no longer needed to complete it. Also, in learning a new task, the body can be awkward and clumsy, and it will use its muscles inefficiently, which takes more energy than when a familiar task can be smoothly done. And yet, some habits are just the things that create these holes in the first place, but these are not so much the habits of things that you do as they are the habits of how you are.

Take for example the simplest things, like how you sit, stand, and move. These require the actions of muscles. And there are ways of sitting, standing, and moving that take far more energy than what is required. Also, within these activities, there are habits of posture that require constant effort, nervous habits of movement that bleed off energy, and habitual constrictions of muscle pairs—for example, the small muscles between the eyebrows that constrict to reduce incoming impressions; the muscles on either side of the jaws that constrict when there is conflict between what one wishes to say but might not feel safe to say; the muscles between the shoulder tops that constrict when bearing psychic burdens, real or imagined; the muscles of the buttocks that constrict while repressing one's instincts; and so on. These are all nothing more than holes in one of your buckets—the one that stores your reserves of mechanical energy.

Now seems as good a time as any to dig a little deeper into this subject of vitality. Imagine a grand cascading fountain, the kind that serves as a centerpiece in any large public park. Picture a tall fountain that gurgles from a single spout at the top of a series of tiers, so that the water from the spout first fills the upper tier and then spills over into the next tier, and when that one fills, the overflow spills into the next tier, and so on.

Now, in your mind, imagine that this is not a fountain of water where gravity acts to pull the flow from top to bottom but a fountain of vitality where the pull is upward, from heaven. This would look like an upside-down fountain—where the gurgle begins at the bottom and the overflow trickles upwards in tiers. This is a view of the arrangement of the buckets that hold our vitality, with the largest bucket at the bottom and the smallest bucket at the top, but this is only an approximate view. It conveys the principle that when a lower bucket is full, its overflow can add a bit to the next bucket above it, and so excess energy never goes to waste.

But this view doesn't convey three important things. First, each bucket has its own independent supply, unique to it alone. So the overflow is, at most, a secondary but important contributor to topping off all but the very first bucket. Second, the accumulations in each of these buckets are fuel of a unique kind, each more rarefied and finer than the fuel in the bucket below it. Each is useful for certain kinds of work but inefficient or even wasteful for other kinds of work. After all, we don't burn diamonds to heat a coal-fired stove. Finally, the energies of attention, awareness, and intent don't fit neatly into any of these buckets but tap into all of them to varying degrees.

Our first bucket contains instinctive energy. This is what fuels all of our bodily functions, and we feel its lack when we are sick. It is a subject of popular culture, so I won't fill this letter with much about it except this: What you put into your body, what you keep out of your body, and what you put your body through, day by day, are the points of leverage in keeping this bucket full. This includes what you eat and drink and what you abstain from consuming; the quality of the air you breathe; the types and qualities of impressions that you absorb through each of your senses, including getting adequate amounts of daylight, having adequate periods of quiet, and getting sufficient sleep. Above all, you must study and learn from your body so that you will learn to read its signals, as these will tell you what you'll need to know to best maintain it.

An exercise to help you get in touch with your reserves of instinctive energy involves learning to move heat around in your body. The exercise has two parts—master the first before trying the second.

In the first part, wait until your feet feel cold. Then go to a sink and turn the hot water on so that it is hotter than warm, but not burning. Put your hands, palms up, into the flow, and when they feel warmed, lift your shoulders up and then drop them quickly, as if you were a bird pumping your wings down. Done correctly, you will sense warmth going down your back, down your calves, and into your feet. Repeat until you have warmed your feet!

The second part of this exercise must be done when you are not feeling particularly cold, but when your hands are cold. Bring your attention to your palms, and with a relaxed intention, work to have your hands heat up. These exercises will get you in touch with your instinctive energy and will also exercise your spiritual muscle of intent.

The next bucket holds your mechanical energy, and this energy is easy to understand. When I have enough, I can move, lift objects, and perform large- and small-scale feats. If I have exhausted my supply, my body will tire, and I will have no choice but to rest.

If food, sleep, and the air I breathe are sufficient, this bucket replenishes itself each and every day. But if I sit with a slouch, my back muscles need to constantly work to support the weight of my head; if I have a nervous twitch with my foot, I bleed this energy out for no good purpose; and if I furrow my brow or tighten my jaws, I sacrifice whatever chance I have to accumulate this fuel and have it added to a bucket of finer vitality.

Mechanical energy is held in a large bucket, because we need a lot of it. Scientists know of this energy, but in the same way that all carbon is not just carbon, molecules of energy contain clouds that can each contain different degrees of synchronization, and for mechanical energy, there is only a simple kind of synchronization. Finer qualities of energy possess synchronizations on deeper levels, but to produce these and so to produce the finer energies, efforts of various kinds are needed. Oh, but I am getting ahead of myself! For now, we just want to patch any holes in your mechanical energy bucket.

The effort needed to patch these holes is like the

effort you have put into rescuing your attention from your thought stream, but here you must first see how you sit, how you stand, how you move, and so on. And you must learn in what ways you can improve. Here it is important to learn a physical discipline with the help of a competent teacher, someone who already possesses good mechanics of posture and movement and who knows how to teach. But before we go into that subject, try this: Imagine yourself standing upright and with good posture, in a way that feels comfortable. I'm sure you can recall a time when you had to stand still and wait in a line, where there really wasn't room to move around, so that your feet stayed exactly where you planted them until it was time to move. The thought of stumbling or falling wouldn't occur to you, as what could be simpler than simply standing still?

But now imagine that the imprints of your feet are used to make for each of them a pedestal that captures your footfalls and the distances between them. The pedestals start off just an inch high, and you step onto them and stand just as before. But now imagine that the pedestals are raised, first two feet off the ground, then ten feet, and then one hundred feet. What happens to your sense of stability? The footfalls are identical—you aren't being forced to balance on a tightrope. But your feeling of security evaporates the higher off the ground you go, despite your foot positions being the same.

The difference is that your instinct recognizes the risk of falling, and this sense overtakes your awareness the higher up you go. Now imagine how you would stand if you were on the highest pedestal. Your foot positions would be the same, but you would be very careful to center your weight on top of your feet, not tip your body, and you would make every effort not to tense up, as that could cause you to topple. Next time you are waiting in line, imagine standing on a towering pedestal. No one needs to know what you are doing. In fact, it is best not to talk about these kinds of exercises or their purpose except in very specific circumstances, but again, I am getting ahead of myself!

I suggest you find a physical discipline that holds your interest—some sport or practice that you are particularly drawn to. The best ones for this purpose contain sets of movements and postures that require discipline and practice to do them well. They must help you strengthen your body, calm your mind, and even out your feelings, and most important, educate your body to gain a sense of rootedness whenever you are standing.

Many activities can fill these requirements. My own preference falls to the martial arts and, in particular, to the practice of Tai Chi Chuan, whose main benefit is to develop this very sense of rootedness. This sense helps in healing endeavors, as the grounding it provides helps to keep one from being taken up by someone else's drama, and in a similar way, it helps in the practice of compassion without sympathy. Also, once you are able to discipline your body so it can be made calm and rooted, you will gain a new sense of vision where, for the first time, you will deeply see the postures and tensions that other people hold.

Regardless of how you develop it, rootedness becomes something like a grounding rod, but having to do with spirit rather than with electricity. There are times when you will be visited by intrusive spirits, and through proper action, you will be able to dispatch some of them through your root. You will need to be able to sense them, you will need to stand in a rooted posture in some natural setting, and you will need to be able to place yourself in a state where your window to heaven is open.

Many of these spirits are attracted to darkness, and so they can be sent into the ground. Just as a bad smell can be removed from your home by opening the front window, opening the back door, and letting a breeze blow through, your window to heaven will let in a breeze, and your rootedness to the earth will open the back door.

But remember, it is far too easy to imagine being capable of these things in advance of actually having these abilities, and this can get you into trouble. Imagination used incorrectly can put the biggest hole in any of your buckets. That itself is another big subject, and if you are interested, we can cover it at another time.

Once you master the basics of your discipline, and if you practice it with diligence, the spirit of this art will visit with you and teach you many meditations to keep your practice fresh.

So that you may understand in what ways a spirit of this kind may offer you help, here are some of the meditations that I have received over the years. On any given day as I move through the Tai Chi postures, I may be prompted to move in a way that least disturbs the air; I may be prompted to focus on always seeing both of my hands within my peripheral vision; I may be prompted to focus on feeling my weight transfer from foot to foot in the way that water is poured slowly from vessel to vessel; I may be prompted to focus on never having any movement stop completely but rather having each movement flow into the next like ocean waves rolling in and out; I may be prompted to focus on feeling the momentum of the movements, even as I stifle that momentum by moving at a slow and steady pace; I may be prompted to perform the movements with my eyes closed and observe all of my body's movements with the eyes of my spirit; I may be prompted to focus on feeling a force enter my body through my root, extend through my body, and exit in a directed way through the palms of my hands; and so on.

Oh, have I ever told you that besides a spirit entering from a window above, there is a spirit of the earth that enters through the soles of your feet? This is the source of the water in the fountain; it starts in the earth and bubbles up! And once you have developed a sense of rootedness and can hold a quiet mind and an open heart, this is where the force will come that will help those sickly plants at your new job!

The practice of a physical discipline, as I have just described, patches many of the holes in the mechanical energy bucket, and at the same time, it also adds energy into it. But you will need an additional form of exercise to top this bucket off if, as with Tai Chi, the intensity is mostly on the inside. You must also practice something that causes you to exert yourself to the maximum degree, even if it is only briefly. Running hard or playing any sport that requires running are the best examples. The goal is to have all of your muscles working hard at the same time. Hard exertion such as this raises you into a higher state. Picture the levels of spirit that I have already described to you, and imagine that with right preparation you will be free to place your awareness within any of these. Hard physical exertion is the preparation needed to enter the spirit of your body's mechanicalness.

Start with conserving your mechanical energy, not through sloth, but instead by disciplining your body into an instrument under your command and by developing a deep and abiding connection between your body and the ground you stand and move on. In this way, your bucket of mechanical energy will no longer leak and, out of its abundance, an overflow will help fill the next bucket above it. And if you are interested, I can tell you about that bucket in my next letter. Do write back soon!

Your loving uncle,
James

On Sex

My Dearest Madeline,

Life gets complicated, eh? There you are tending the seedlings that got off to a tough start and witnessing the benefits of your ministrations, when suddenly you are distracted and wonder if you could be falling in love! Yes, the nursery owner's son sounds like a fine young fellow, but now I understand that this new circumstance is at the heart of the obstacles you face. My dear, allow me to lay your concerns to rest. These events are fortunate for you, but not for the reason you are thinking These complications are giving you a direct experience you'll never forget. A lesson in how it feels when there are leaks in some of your buckets, because when there is confusion, buckets are leaking.

You describe a mutual attraction between the two of you, but you also wrote how hurt you felt when he ignored you while he was among his friends, and you expressed doubts that his feeling for you might not be the same as your feeling for him. We can view all of this from the point of view of your buckets of vitality, as we are in the midst of these already.

The *falling* of *falling in love*, when it is not a choice made with your intent, the strength of your awareness, and your integrity in accordance with the highest kind of love, pokes holes in every one of your buckets. But rather, if this is a choice made with your eyes wide open, it can lead to a mutual patching and mutual filling of one another's buckets. So, either way, the stakes are high.

As it so happens, this circumstance has its greatest effects, either positively or negatively, on the next two buckets we have yet to consider—the one housing your sexual energy and the one housing your emotional energy. Leaks in these buckets are the subjects of great literature and art, but we will look at them simply, from the point of view of how to keep them from leaking. Once you understand this, you will no longer be confused, but instead, you will be able to make conscious decisions. Then falling in love will not be like having your pocket picked, but instead, you will be choosing if you wish to open your purse.

Now is as good a time as any to explore the nature of these two particular buckets. Unlike the others, not only is the character of the energies within them unique, but these buckets are prone to leak in some very particular ways.

The bucket containing sexual energy, particularly at your age, my dear, is like a germinating seed in that it sprouts roots that grow into each of your other buckets. No other bucket does this. But God in heaven made it this way so that if conditions of life make survival dire, all energies can assist with procreation. But this unique structure is like a two-edged sword, because these roots are each like a two-way street! It is not just that the bucket of sexual energy can tap into each of the other buckets to gain vitality; the flow can go the other way, and sexual energy can be lost to any of the other buckets, as easily as if they were sipping soda through a straw. But that kind of flow tends to be deleterious to the soul.

Consider in the normal course of events, an overflow of sexual energy simply bubbles upward and adds to the bucket of emotional energy, bestowing on it a certain edge. If that bucket overflows and, in the normal course of things, it too bubbles upward, then the buckets above it become enriched. This happy turn of events can lead to the highest expressions of which the human soul is capable, one of which can be the creation of an enduring link to the spirit of healing. But take an example where the sexual energy bucket sends a root upward to the buckets that reside in the thinking parts of the brain, bypassing the tempering that comes about from the more natural pathway of sexual energy first mixing with emotional energy. This new pathway can, in dire circumstances, ensure adequate sexual energy for procreation. But if the flow goes the other way, then the thinking parts feed directly off of sexual energy, without the tempering effect of emotional energy. The unfortunate results of this are obsessions in the mind about sex, which can lead to a kind of insanity.

As for sexual energy itself, it has four main qualities, and it will be good for you to understand a bit about each of them, because, my dear, at your age, there is so very much of an unbalanced view on what is thought of as sex.

First, this energy has a magnetic quality that seeks out its polar opposite in all different kinds of relations in order to balance out its nature. Polar love, that is, love of one who, magnetically, feels like one's opposite in one or more ways, has many different forms. The fact that opposites attract even among one's casual friends is simply a result of the magnetic action of sexual energy.

Second, this energy helps one to persevere in the face of the unknown. The captain of a ship, navigating dangerous waters and through a bank of fog, has all of his senses on highest alert. His persistent attention, tuned to its highest level to avoid running aground, is fed by this quality of sexual energy. In the same way, a scientist pursuing a new discovery through uncharted waters taps into this same source for sustenance. In its simplest form, imagine for a moment the life of a single sperm cell, swimming blind, upstream, and among two hundred million others, searching for an egg to fertilize and pressing on despite the odds against it!

Third, this energy has the capacity to form a safe and nurturing home. When a group of people are working toward the same goal, whether they are in a church, a business, on a sporting team, in a theatrical production, or performing medical research, things go better if the head of the group can channel this aspect of his or her sexual energy. It creates an environment of inclusion, non-judgment, safety, and a place for all to grow individually and as a group.

In the same way, think of the work your cousin does in the animal shelter, nursing the orphaned and the sick. Her success there is tied to her capacity to use a portion of her sexual energy in this way. Perhaps you know the biblical story of the woman suffering from a hemorrhage, who touched the garment worn by the Christian Lord, and as she was healed, He felt that virtue had gone out of him. This is an accurate description of sexual energy transformed into the healing energy known as virtue. And finally, of course, think of the womb and what it can do.

Fourth, this energy doesn't flow as a steady stream; it accumulates to a particular intensity, and then it erupts all at once; think of Old Faithful, the famous geyser. This is what produces the experience known as *orgasm*, but there are more subtle ways that this aspect of sexual energy finds expression. Any sudden insight, any "Aha!" moment, any creative revelation that comes not through plodding reason but, instead, comes through in a flash, is connected to having sexual energy sufficiently present to create a pressure that can then, in a burst, lead to illumination.

The bucket containing emotional energy was designed by God to be shallower than it ought to be, so it easily overflows upward. This shallow bucket is the "cup" in the Psalm that "runneth over." It was made shallow so that emotional energy would be shared, overflowing upward into buckets we have yet to consider. So by its nature, it tends to be a very leaky bucket. Can you imagine how easy it might be to lose great pools of this vitality?

My dearest niece, now you find yourself on the crest of womanhood, feeling with your soul that same pull that so captivated me when I was young—the pull to bring a spirit of healing into one's inner and outer world. But at the same time, feeling with your body the pull of another kind of attraction. And while these may not be incompatible, you must be careful in love, as it can be the easiest way to lose more of your vitality than you can possibly imagine.

And you, my dear, are at tremendous risk in this

regard. Having lost your father and your brother[16] while you were so very young has left you without a palate in your heart for the taste of the polar love from a man who has no desire to possess you. You were fortunate to have met Simon, as he did much to secure your heart,[17] but still you are vulnerable. You must be particularly careful with regards to your sexual relations. It is far too common for those in your shoes to see in the amorous advances of a fine young fellow the answer to a hunger for the kind of polar love that you largely lost out on. Yet, for the young fellow, it may simply be a wish to possess you, finding your polarity attractive to his body but not necessarily interested in engaging your heart.

The sex act itself mingles souls together. So if you have yet to curate your own soul, how much harder will it be if you then need to curate the spirits of this other soul that would then be joined within yours? And in this age of casual sex when young people accumulate legions of spirits from the uncurated souls from each of their partners, the emotional energy bucket, in an

---

16   *The Charm Carver*, p 55.
17   Ibid., p 89.

effort to protect itself from all of this spurious input, builds a wall around itself, and the heart, as they say, hardens.

Also, for a woman, each sex partner pokes a new, unique hole in her sexual energy bucket: the more partners, the more potential leaks. If the emotional energy bucket did not wall itself up, it would drain downward and exhaust itself in an effort to replenish the leaky bucket below. So, if you wish to cultivate a spirit of healing, the sex act can never be a casual thing. The heart must not be forced to wall itself in, because if it does, it will lose its sense of compassion, and then the spirit of healing will not find in you a welcome home.

It is worth mentioning that the reason that the act of sex pokes a hole in a woman's sexual energy bucket is that God designed it this way to create an opening for a new soul to enter the womb. But whenever sexual union brings together two loving souls, it is the love within that union that patches the hole and keeps the vitality from leaking out. But without love, there is no patch. Worse still is, if the intent behind the sex act is dishonest, selfish, or violent, then the hole in the sexual energy bucket becomes, by degrees, a wound that won't heal without a great deal of love—first, love for one's own integrity and, second, help from the love of another soul.

So you see, my dear, there is a danger for you in this type of union if it is not filled with a generous love. Without love, a sexual union will drain your sexual energy and your emotional energy from you, and your heart will harden to protect itself. Where can a spirit of healing find a welcome home when all the vitality, normally bubbling upward, is instead cascading downward through a series of buckets and holes?

So, my dearest, be careful in love; develop a taste for love without possession, and before you engage in sexual relations, ask yourself four questions: Do I love him? Does he love me? Does he respect me? And, Do I trust him? These will assure that, even if this love is lost, your heart will not be broken, and your vitality will not run out of you like water through a channel poked in an earthen dam.[18]

Now seems as good a time as any to clear up your question about receiving a spirit of healing or, for that matter, any other facet of the love of God that comes down to us from heaven. Imagine for a moment that

---

18   *The Charm Carver*, p 60.

you are out in a field on a dark, moonless night, and you have with you a flashlight that casts a bright and narrow ray of light. Imagine that you point this ray upward. No one will see it, but in time, it will attract moths, who will flutter and dance in the light.

The moths are like the facets of the love of God that come down to us, on their own. We don't have to chase them, and we don't have to run around with a net to snare them; they are free to us. But how can they find us? We need to be like the ray of light, as this is what attracts them. And for us, if we can clean house and have our vitality overflow from the bottom to the top, it radiates upward through the tops of our heads like the flashlight ray pointed to the sky. This is how any of us create an enduring link with the spirit of healing. It follows the ray of our vitality right into our hearts.

Of course, space must be made in your heart by cultivating a spirit of compassion. Your buckets must not leak very much, to assure sufficient quantity, and the quality of your vitality must be fine enough to attract the higher spirits of perception. Then, as long as the energies in your brain are also in accord, your vitality will cast a beacon that will form an enduring link.

Regarding holes in your emotional energy bucket, here are some exercises for you to try:

1. Be cautious about gushing emotionally; it needlessly depletes your heart. It is not always important to let others know how you feel. This doesn't mean that you should pretend you are not feeling as you are or that you should suppress yourself from feeling certain things. Experience everything, but choose carefully what you wish to express outwardly as, to do so, you must open your purse and pay.

2. Be cautious about going on and on in talking and in writing. There is great power that accumulates when you hold onto an idea, a plan, or a creative endeavor. Let it ripen within you rather than letting the force of this bleed out through casual exchange. It is for this reason that I have cautioned you that when practicing any of the exercises I have suggested, do not casually speak about them to anyone. Instead, resist that outward flow, and in this way your bucket will fill all the more.

3. Be cautious of any appetite that turns into a vice. Things consumed through any of the senses can easily tap into the emotional energy bucket. And unless bridled by your own wish to contain your vitality, any of these can form holes in that bucket, which, after all, is just what a vice really is.

4. Practice love without possession, a love where you expect nothing in return. This goes along with practicing compassion without sympathy, which is tied to your rootedness. And along with these, practice putting yourself into the shoes of another; see if you can learn to see and understand a person from their own point of view, but again, without losing yourself in the process.

I don't think I mentioned that we group vitality into these buckets because it reflects our common experience. Different kinds of work deplete different kinds of energy, and when you have exhausted one particular bucket, you will still be able to do other kinds of work from buckets that have not been exhausted. Right now, my mechanical energy is near exhaustion, as I had a long and grueling day, but I am able to enter into your feelings, as my emotional energy remains strong, and I can share these ideas with you, as the energies of my thinking brain have yet to be depleted today.

We have a few more buckets to go, if you are still interested, but for now, this is enough for you to digest, my dearest. I look forward to hearing back from you soon.

Your loving uncle,
James

On Imagination

My Dearest Madeline,

It is easy for me to forget just how fast things change for the young! I wouldn't have imagined that in the span of a single month you would go from working in a nursery and dealing with questions of love to gaining a sense from the depths of your being of what you wish to do in your life. I am not surprised by this fortunate turn of events, as I believe that this wish of yours lay in wait as a seed beneath the winter ground, waiting for the warmth of the sun to call it forth. For you, that warmth came from your vitality, no longer leaking, but rising like a fountain and freeing you to see what was hidden all along.

It is often a chance encounter over matters just mildly consequential that end up changing the course of one's life. When Simon sent you to see the Moon Lake Woman, it was for an answer to just such a question.[19] Who would have guessed at your enchantment with the rhythms of her loom? But fate is like that. It dangles possibilities before our eyes every single day, but it is not every single day that we have the strength to see these things for what they truly are. Instead, these appear as a mass of patterns, with no single part attracting the eye.[20] It is only if, as Simon said, "we store sufficient strength to form an inner wish,"[21] that any part of these rise in bold relief and form for us a vision, rich with meaning.

This revelation is fortunate for you for reasons beyond illuminating your path, as it has given you direct experience, as all revelations do, of what is possible when all of your buckets, including the three we have yet to discuss, even briefly become leak-free.

---

19 *The Charm Carver*, pp 67–72.
20 Ibid., pp 53, 75.
21 Ibid., pp 59–65.

This experience shows that you have patched the buckets we have already covered. But it also shows that, even without a clear understanding, you briefly managed to patch the remaining three buckets that reside in your head. The fact is, one or another of these buckets is leaking almost all of the time, and they only remain patched with the vigilance of a quiet mind.

But in moments however brief, when all of the patches hold, all vitality becomes contained and beams up to heaven as a kind of silent prayer. And this becomes the channel for every kind of revelation.

It will be useful for you to learn a bit about each of these last three buckets. With a clear understanding, it will be easier to recreate this inner alignment that has enabled you to glimpse through the eyes of your soul. But first, I will tell you the tale of the king and his three doctors.

A wise, old king knew he was dying, and he was suffering greatly. He had his noblemen scour his kingdom to bring him the three doctors who all agreed were the finest in the land. One by one, the king asked each of them for their recommendation.

The first doctor was well known and well liked. He took one look at the king and said, "Your Majesty,

I know just what you have; I have seen this a thousand times, and I have written about this very thing in my newly published book. I recommend that you follow the instructions in it, and you'll be better in no time." And he handed the king a signed copy of his brand-new book but then left so quickly that the king did not have a chance to even utter a word to him.

The second doctor was known to be thoughtful. He thoroughly examined the king and then told him, "You have a very complicated condition, but there are some experimental treatments that are showing prom-ise. I recommend that we take you to our hospital, where we can do many tests and begin your treatment." The king thanked him and told him that he would think about this recommendation.

The third doctor was known for her kindness and wisdom. She sat beside the king and took his wrist in order to study his pulse; she held his wrist in silence for a quarter of an hour. Was she just taking his pulse, or was she doing something else? And if she was doing something else, it could not be discerned by any of his servants; they wondered if perhaps she was doing nothing at all.

Then she put down his wrist and gazed into his

eyes for a very long time and said to him, "Prepare a great feast for your subjects, and allow all who wish to, to come forward and share with you how your reign has helped them in their lives. For your suffering is nothing more than that of a lover, aching with the knowledge that soon he will depart from his beloved. You must hear from your kingdom, in the chorus of their own voices, of their love for you and their feeling that, because of you, even once you're gone, they will all be well and will not soon forget you."

And the king thanked this doctor, ordered up the feast, and at the height of those festivities, announced that with his passing, this doctor would reign as queen of the land.

These doctors differed in the energies they held in these three remaining buckets, and this determines what kind of imagination they could each afford to pay for. You see, my dearest, nothing illustrates the nature of the three remaining buckets better than a clear understanding of just what imagination is or what it can be.

Imagine you are away, but at a familiar place, and you begin your journey home. Hasn't it ever happened that you arrive at home and can't recall a thing about your journey? Your mind may have been busy, and the path you took was so familiar that it left not a trace. Here, your imagination was a kind of premade map that kept you pointed in the right direction, all the way home. In the same way, haven't you ever found yourself telling the same story for the hundredth time, and once you start telling it, it practically tells itself? In these instances, there is an automatic retrieval of something already stored that simply plays out, with no effort or awareness on your part. The first doctor was only able to muster imagination from this lowest of the three remaining buckets.

This bucket contains the energy we use for all forms of automatic thinking. It is always the case that the activity of this energy never leaves a trace in our awareness. It is solely involved with thinking without learning; new memories can't be made with this energy, and we can have no recollection of any action, thought, or feeling that results from the use of this energy alone. And because the use of this energy never leaves a trace, it is possible to live in a delusion, where I believe I am having an original thought—even though this thought of mine was put there, years ago, by somebody else. Or I believe that I am having an authentic feeling, even though I am only retrieving something rather dusty, from the back of an old drawer.

The energy of automatic thinking is of great help to us. It streamlines activities so we don't need to remember how to accomplish things we've done many times before. In the best of circumstances, it is used often but sparingly, as one would ask a librarian for help in finding a reference. It sets the patterns for making breakfast, and walking the dog, and such. And these kinds of activities are a great refuge from intensive work. But when used to excess, this bucket is drained, and the two above it, linked tightly together as they are, can never stay filled. This happens if we live an unexamined life—a life without the hunger of curiosity or the wish for new learning. This is imagination without consciousness, and it can be a kind of hell.

This bucket also leaks when we live our lives as if we are just going through the motions. Living in this way, we can only have mechanical habits of feeling, not the true emotions that come from the heart and arrive in a flash without words or story. For many poor souls, these habits of feeling are their only experience of emotions. But true emotions are prompted from below, from instinct, or from above, from heaven, and never form from a thought. Habits of feeling are nothing more than colorations of well-worn thoughts—such as worry, anxiety, and fear, which lead to the endless ruminations that drain this bucket dry.

Now imagine that I have asked you to give me directions to your home, but I am unfamiliar with your town, and I am coming into it from a direction that you don't often use. Also, I prefer a route that will take me past the most beautiful places so that I can take in the sights. And lastly, because of a problem with my steering wheel, I can only make right-hand turns. So though you are familiar with your town, you have to think through each of these issues, and once you have the route in your head, you've got to visualize the whole trip, step by step, so that you can explain it to someone who doesn't know your town at all.

Using the mind's eye to visualize these kinds of details and assembling them in a way that you have never done before requires a kind of active imagination that can never be automatic. This kind of imagination is paid for with energy from the middle bucket, and it was this kind of imagination used by the second doctor.

Learning anything new and creating new connections between things that you already know are actions that stem from this active-thinking energy. If you have ever spent time doing intensive learning or problem solving, you will know that this bucket will only hold so much. Once you have reached the bottom, you will not be able to visualize anything new. Instead, you will need to rest and allow more energy of this kind to accumulate. That rest can come from sleep, or it can come from activities that you can do automatically and without thinking. But one thing that you can do to help replenish this energy faster is to perform some automatic task, like making breakfast, but attend to it while you are doing it. Don't just go through the motions mindlessly, but pay reverent attention to everything you are doing. Make breakfast as if the choreography of making breakfast were a speeded-up form of Tai Chi Chuan, and observe your movements in the ways that I described to you in a previous letter. It is remarkable how effective this exercise is in replenishing this energy.

This bucket leaks whenever you repeatedly call upon it to assemble scenarios that don't jive with reality. Fantasies, conspiracy theories, and the like are worthwhile if you wish to write novels. And if you have a legitimate dream, this energy will put meat on

the bones of it. But if you are pretending to be someone who you are not or living in a way that is inauthen-
tic, then you are constantly calling upon this energy to
visualize versions of yourself that it will diligently com-
pare with what it knows to be true, and it will burn
through its energy as it struggles to reconcile these dis-
crepancies. This energy doesn't come cheaply!

Simon once commented on this, telling me in his
poetic way, "I apportion my surmise as a miser counts
his coins."[22] So to keep this bucket from leaking, be
responsible for your actions. Be consistent with who
you are, and honor your commitments. Don't be reck-
less with money, be current with any of your debts,
value what is true and honest, and always let your word
be your bond.

Now imagine that you are trying to solve a problem
that is difficult in an entirely different way from giving
me driving directions. For example, think of how you
would inform your mother that you initiated contact
with me! I'm not suggesting you do this, as it may be
best to leave things as they are without burdening her
with the old conflict between your father and me. But

---

22   *The Charm Carver*, p 75.

by thinking this through, you will come up against her point of view, and if you were to try and change it, you'd need to be creative. So thinking it through would only get you so far. What you would really need would be some kind of inspiration that would show you, through wisdom and compassion, a process, maybe a gradual one, where eventually it would become just a small step to share your renewed contact with me with her.

Where does that kind inspiration come from? It certainly can't come from the same place that planning a driving route comes from. Instead it must come from the highest form of imagination that we are capable of, just short of revelation. This comes from the energy in our topmost bucket, the energy that pays for inspired imagination and this is the imagination that the king's third doctor was capable of using.

This is the smallest bucket of all, and it only ever holds a limited quantity of energy. It is filled by what trickles up to it: some from the overall flow of the whole fountain, most from the overflow of just the two other buckets in the head and, perhaps most important, from a reverse flow of any excess traveling upwards through the root formed by the sexual energy bucket.

It is not so much that this highest bucket leaks; it is just that all the other buckets can't themselves be leaking if there is ever to be any accumulation in it. Your house must be clean, my dearest, for there to be available to you a ready supply from this tiny upper bucket. I've already given you many exercises to help you clean house, but if there is a single one that is essential in accumulating in this bucket, it is practicing silence in the mind. If your automatic-thinking or your active-thinking energies are being used, there will not be a drop to spare for trickling upward. Remember in the tale of the king how long the third doctor spent, silently sensing his pulse and silently gazing into his eyes?

And so, my dearest, now you know about all of the buckets and have even had a glimpse of revelation. So I would be remiss if I didn't, at least briefly, cover the subject of prayer. All too often, prayers are memorized as a series of words and are recited strictly from automatic thinking. No good can come from this, as true prayer must engage what is not automatic. Words alone can't create the inner alignment needed to patch up all the buckets. Effort must be brought to bear to radiate our vitality up to heaven. Then grace will enter us with ease.

Real prayer can bring a greater synchronization to living things but also to substances, objects, and structures. And while nothing can store a spirit of healing, as it can only flow like a blowing breeze, things can be made to hold a spirit of healing in the same way that a bell holds its ring. Had I understood this years ago, I could have changed the nature of that angry loaf of bread that made me so ill. With your interest now in weaving, ponder how you might bring a spirit of healing into your workspace and into each and every piece that will come from your loom. This is a big subject, but if you are interested, we can cover it at another time.

Just one more thing—about you leaving the nursery for the better pay of waiting tables, to better help with the costs of buying your loom. I consider waiting tables to be a treasure for anyone wishing to bring a spirit of healing into their work. It educates the body to be efficient with movement, it educates the mind to be attentive and focused, and it educates one's feelings to accept challenges with grace. Your tips will mostly reflect your success in these lessons. But when they don't, as some café patrons could care less about the help, this lack will give you a lesson in humbleness that no one who wishes to work with a spirit of healing ought to be without.

I look forward to hearing all about your weaving!

Your loving uncle,
James

On Reverence

My Dearest Madeline,

I smiled at your wish to apprentice with the Moon Lake Woman. As it happens, I know her well. I tended to her husband at the end of his life[23] and spent a great deal of time with the two of them.

It is always best to wait for a teacher to recognize something in you, rather than asking, unbidden, for an apprenticeship. My advice is to go to her with the intent of purchasing one of her weavings, and while you are there, find a good question to ask her.

---

23   *The Charm Carver*, p 72.

For the Moon Lake Woman, a good question is food for her soul,[24] but it must be a very good question for it to stir her interest in you. I can't tell you what to ask, but I can tell you some things about her and her work that will help.

The first time I met the Moon Lake Woman, it was in her work studio. When I arrived, she was at her loom with her back to the door; I couldn't see her face, and she did not acknowledge my entrance, though she knew that I was there.

Like you, I was enchanted by the rhythms of her loom. I heard music: jingles when she treadled the frames, forming all her patterns; a swish when she tossed her shuttle, threading in a row; and slaps when she beat the weft, tight against her weaving. "Jingle-swish-slap-jingle-slap! Jingle-swish-slap-jingle-slap!" It was almost as if a weaving machine was doing this, except every so often, the rhythm would change almost imperceptibly. If you weren't closely listening, you'd not hear these little changes.

Later, I asked her about these, and she told me

---

24   *The Charm Carver*, p 87.

that in those changes, small intricacies found their way into her patterns.

She said, "A loom can be just a weaving machine. If I only work with mechanical skill, the result will be skillfully made cloth, no better than if it were made by a machine. But a loom allows for other things. With it, I can bring a mood, a wish, or a prayer into my weaving."

And I asked her if she could tell me more about this, as it was a subject that interested me greatly. And she was silent for a moment, and then she said, "It is easy to bring a mood into a weaving. I can do this by choosing patterns, textures, and colors that seem to fit the mood. Then I just need to align my heart with the spirit of this mood, and as I weave, somehow, it finds its way into the cloth.

"A wish is a bit harder, as the patterns, textures, and colors for any particular wish are not as obvious as they are for a mood. And if I am to hold a wish as I weave, I must be better aligned, as the spirit of a wish lives partly in my heart and partly in my head.

"A prayer is the hardest of all to bring into a weaving, and often when I am asked to make something with a prayer in it, the person is really only after a wish.

Few understand what prayer really is: It is an open channel to heaven! To bring prayer into a weaving, I must be reverently aligned. And in this state, I choose the pattern, the textures, and the colors. And in this state, I sit at my loom, and with no words, I listen. And in this state, I weave. And somehow, the prayer finds its way into the cloth."

She invited me to stay in her studio while she went to tend to her husband. He was, by then, bedridden, and I had just seen him before I came to meet with her. At her suggestion, I sat at her loom while she was away; the room was quiet, and a bit of the morning sun shone through a window facing out to Moon Lake.

As the quiet of the room enveloped me, I sensed the profundity of this quiet. It was clear that this room held no residue of disharmony, no traces of contentiousness, argument, drama, or pointless talk. But prayer, yes. And just as she had described bringing prayers into her weavings, the walls and even the loom itself seemed to hold a sacredness.

I had felt something similar years before, when I visited a monastery. There, prayers had so entered the stones of the structure that it made it easy to connect with heaven. The prayers had brought finer synchronizations deep into every grain of every stone, and in the way that a magnet aligns a piece of iron, I became aligned with those centuries of prayer.

When the Moon Lake Woman returned, I asked her about this feeling in her space; could she tell me anything about it? She paused for a moment, and then said, "I have only ever used this room for my work. It has never had another purpose, so when I began, it was very much a clean slate. When I first started weaving, I was young and inexperienced, and I was lucky to find work making towels for dishes. But that was how I learned the mechanics of my craft.

"At that time, I began to notice a mood within this room when I came in in the morning: It was a feeling of serious industry. That was my feeling whenever I worked, and gradually the spirit of this mood made a home in this space. So even when I would just walk in, my studio brought me into the mood to weave!

"Later on, once I was known as a skilled weaver, I began to get requests for pieces to carry certain moods. I did wall hangings for children's bedrooms, happy pieces and things like that. And the more of those that I did, the more this room began to resonate with the feelings of those pieces.

"Later still, as my reputation grew, I began to get requests for wishes. And it brought me back to when Simon carved my charm.[25] Many times, he told me, 'A charm is but a wish, confined.'[26] And the spirits of common wishes—for health, for happiness, for success—began to inhabit my walls. I was calling upon them often, and so they made themselves at home.

"But these days, most of my requests are for weavings filled with prayer, and this now suits me. Some who ask for prayers really just want a wish, and I send them to another weaver. With my husband's life so near its end, wishing will not change a thing for me. But I have taken great solace in prayer, working in a prayerful state, living as reverently as I am able, and trying to bring as much sacredness into every moment and into each of my weavings as I am capable of doing."

And I asked her if she could show me a finished weaving that had a prayer in it, and she produced a shawl meant to be worn while praying. She placed it over my shoulders, and all at once, I sensed a silence, an

---

25   *The Charm Carver*, pp 71-72.
26   Ibid., pp 42, 88.

alignment, and after a moment, that feeling so familiar to me of a spirit of healing entering my heart.

And I asked the Moon Lake Woman one more thing: Did she have any sense of how this prayer of hers got into her weaving? Did she work her weft in an intricate way at those moments when the music of her loom varied in its rhythms? And she told me she knew none of those things. To her, it was not a thing to know. It was a way of being.

All that was knowable, she explained, was to be reverent without end.

So, you see, my dearest niece, the Moon Lake Woman is more than a weaver of cloth! And with your interest being what it is, I can't imagine a more perfect pairing than the two of you. When you see her, please give her my fondest regards.

And write once you've gone to her, and tell me how it went!

Your loving uncle,
James

On Dying & Living

My Dearest Madeline,

Life is full of circles, isn't it? Your brief encounter, years ago, with the Moon Lake Woman has now brought you to an apprenticeship! What a beautiful circle. It doesn't surprise me that she is taking you under her wing. She knows she can make a difference in your growth, and at this point in her life, that is important to her. But you did surprise me when you told me where you had set up your loom.

I had never seen the shop that Simon set up in that

cottage,[27] but you told me so much about your time there that I can well imagine it. How unusual, after all these years, that no one else had ever rented it out. And how fortunate for you that the landlord, happy for a tenant at last, gave you such generous terms!

So now this space, still holding Simon's intentions, will be the home of your own ardent efforts. Another beautiful circle! And what a wonderful blanket you have woven for me. I am honored that you've given me the first fruits of your labor, and I will treasure it for the rest of my life.

Like another circle closing, your need for my advice is coming to an end, my dear. The Moon Lake Woman will now be the one to answer your call. My last bit of advice to you is to keep the spirit of your work space clean. In the same way that you have managed to clean house within your own soul, you must be equally careful with the moods and the spirits that you invite and allow into your space.

It must become and remain your own little church, your own place of worship. As it will be there that you will spend many hours and days, focusing your intent,

---

27   *The Charm Carver*, pp 29, 35, 81, 85, 88, 89.

the strength of your awareness and your integrity, all to be in accord with the highest kind of love. Cultivate your space, and when your vitality slackens, it will give to you an extra measure of strength. Make and keep it sacred, and it will fortify your soul.

Now I must share with you something I have not shared with you before. My own circle, the circle of this life of mine is coming to a close. Because of my profession, I was aware of the signs even before my vitality began to dissipate like the outflowing tide. And I am learned enough to know just how few are the days that remain for me.

Please don't fret! You used to do so much of that, and you've come so very far. Working for years with the dying has taught me their secret: Live every day as if you are dying, for we all surely are. Work to see in the faces of those all around you that each of them have numbered days, and treat everyone as if you may never see them again.

I have no fear of what confronts me; I have cultivated my soul from out of the countless threads of spirit that God has put before me. Those have been the warp of my innermost garment, and I have spent my life laying down the weft, day by day and row by row, weaving my soul into a sturdy vessel that will carry my awareness beyond the reaches of time.

And now my garment is all but complete. And if I am able, I should like to spend the next measure of eternity resting in the walls of your newly forming home. From there, I shall be able to offer you help from time to time. Not advice any longer, but help of quite a different sort.

My dearest, as you work your loom, listen to its music and attune to every rhythm and change. I'll be there, helping your prayers to nest within your weavings. The spirit of healing is with you now. Let it be the weft within the garment of your soul, and weave it through the fibers that stretch across your loom. Be reverent, always and in everything, and in the midst of that reverence, there you will find me.

Your loving uncle,

James

Acknowledgments

With a grateful heart, I wish to acknowledge those sources and individuals who, together but across space and time, contributed to my understanding, synthesis, and writing of this book.

For my understanding of the great questions of life, I wish to thank the ancient authors of the books of the Bible, in particular the Books of Wisdom in the Old Testament and much of the New Testament. Also, from the distant past, I have gained much from the teachings of Lau-Tzu (Taoist), Basho (Zen Buddhist), and Rumi and Hafiz (Sufi).

Among more recent sources, I wish to acknowledge Brother Lawrence's book, *The Practice of the Presence of God* that says so much in a very small space, Kahlil Gibran who taught me how words can be made to heal, and C. S. Lewis, who, in *The Screwtape Letters,* gave me the idea of wrapping this complex teaching in the blanket of a story told through letters.

Among contemporary sources, I wish to acknowledge the philosophical and practical teachings of Rudolph Steiner, George Gurdjieff, Peter Ouspensky, and Carlos Castenada; the scientific explorations of Masaru Emoto, William Tiller, Rupert Sheldrake, Vernon Neppe, Edward Close, and Claude Swanson, and a special thanks to the person who has and continues to be the standard bearer for tirelessly educating the scientific and medical community that consciousness is a foundational force in the universe and not simply a phenomenon generated by neurons in the brain, the physician, author, and editor, Dr. Larry Dossey. Also, I would be remiss if I did not also acknowledge the inspirational effect that the music of the late jazz musician John Coltrane has had on me, as well as the jazz piano music of Keith Jarrett.

Among my personal teachers, I wish to acknowledge my martial arts instructors, Sensei Joe Turchiano (Judo) and Master Don Ahn (Tai Chi, meditation, oriental brush painting), and my other personal guides: Pierce Wheeler, William Segal, and Michel de Saltzmann (meditation, presence of being, attention).

I also owe a debt of gratitude to a group of individuals who, in different ways and at different times, encouraged me to shape this book into the form you have before you: Bernie Siegel, MD, Tamara Iwaseczko, Lori Liddy, Neli Lozej, Florinda Mattia, Marcie Schaeffler, Frankie Timmers, and Laura Trisiano.

Lastly, no one has had more of a hand in shaping my understanding of the world, both without and within, than my wife and partner, Mary.

ABOUT THE AUTHOR

David Shuch has published two other books: *Doctor, Be Well: Integrating the Spirit of Healing with Scientific Medicine* (1stBooks, 2003) and *The Charm Carver* (Integrative Arts Press, 2005). He is a practicing dentist and the founder and director of The Center for Integrative Dentistry, in northwestern New Jersey (www.centerforintegrativedentistry.com), near where he lives with his wife and their companion animals.